How to Influence
Others at Work

How to Influence Others at Work

Psychoverbal communication
for managers

Second Edition

Dick McCann

Butterworth–Heinemann Ltd
Linacre House, Jordan Hill, Oxford OX2 8DP

🌐 PART OF REED INTERNATIONAL BOOKS

OXFORD   LONDON   BOSTON
MUNICH   NEW DELHI   SINGAPORE   SYDNEY
TOKYO   TORONTO   WELLINGTON

First published 1988
First published as a paperback edition 1989
Reprinted 1990
Second edition 1993

© Team Management International Ltd 1988, 1993

British Library Cataloguing in Publication Data
McCann, Dick
    How to influence others at work: psychoverbal
    communication for managers – 2nd rev. ed.
    I. Title
    658.4'5

ISBN 0 7506 0990 7

Phototypeset by Deltatype Ltd, Ellesmere Port, Cheshire
Printed and bound in Great Britain by Redwood Press Ltd, Melksham, Wiltshire

Contents

Preface to Second Edition

Since writing this book five years ago the concept of Team Management Systems (TMS) has gone from strength to strength. TMS and the associated software is now available in over twenty different countries and in eight different languages.

This book is an extension of the TMS concept applied to the field of communication and has now been translated into French and Danish. The ideas I wrote about five years ago have now become well established in management development programmes throughout the world.

To help people develop their influencing skills when interacting with others I have recently developed the Influencing Skills Index and associated software. Respondents answer forty questions about a person they wish to 'influence' and a 3000–4000 word report is produced giving guidance on the seven key influencing skills – *pacing*, *enquiry*, *diagnosis*, *summarizing*, *leading*, *proposing*, and *persuading*. The software and materials are available from the TMS distributors listed at the end of the book.

In this second edition I have added a new chapter on communication channels. This chapter has developed from the various influencing skills workshops I have run and gives practical guidance on how to improve 'awareness' in the various visual, auditory, and kinesthetic communication channels.

Dick McCann
Brisbane, December 1992

Preface

In 1982 I started collaborating with Charles Margerison, trying to answer some of the questions about management development that had been consistently presented to us in our work as management educators. As a result of that collaboration, we produced a set of training materials known as the Team Management Resource, which is now in use throughout the world in more than twelve countries and 200 organizations.

In the last four years, as a result of teaching and training over 1000 managers personally, I have taken our original Team Management work and attempted to use it to answer further questions that many managers have asked me. The common recurrent theme put to me is 'How can we use our knowledge about the differences between people to make us better communicators and therefore, managers?'

In attempting to answer this question I decided to base my work on the findings of John Grinder and Richard Bandler, who in the mid-1970s developed the techniques which have become known as *neuro-linguistic programming*. I consider their work to be one of the most significant developments in the field of interpersonal relationships during the last decade. I admire their work and am indebted to them.

In writing this book I have combined many of the techniques of neuro-linguistic programming with the work of Carl Jung, who was the original inspiration for the Team Management Resource. The result is a new look at interpersonal communication – one that I have called Psychoverbal Communication.

There are many people who have helped me in this book. In particular I would like to thank my friend and colleague Charles Margerison for the thought-provoking ideas he has raised in the course of our many conversations. I have used his categorization of conversations into 'Problem-centred' and 'Solution-centred' as the starting point for the Psychoverbal Communication model.

I am a 'Creator-Innovator', and you will note when you read this book that they have a tendency to start many things but finish few. Therefore I am particularly indebted to my friends at Hewlett-Packard in California – Bruno Dalbiez and Daniel Jeanrenaud – who, by their enthusiasm and interest in my work, have inspired me to complete this book.

Finally, thanks to my wife and family, who have been a 'testing ground' for many of my techniques. This book is dedicated to them – to Dianne, Tim, Kirsty, Rowan and Tessa.

I have used the masculine gender throughout this book where it has not been possible to use neutral plural pronouns. This is not because I am sexist but because filling a text with he/she or him/her interferes with logical thought processes. Wherever the masculine gender is used the female gender equally applies.

Dick McCann
Brisbane, April 1988

1

Conversations – successes and failures

Last night I was at a party. I had gathered up a drink and was quietly standing in a corner watching three people in conversation. Actually only two were talking; poor old Jim was wedged between Debbie and Barbara and was making some effort to communicate with them. Jim was a good friend of mine – a man of few words but very knowledgeable, witty and interesting to talk to. Barbara and Debbie were also friends – both gregarious and outspoken. I craned my neck forwards and overheard the following conversation –

Barbara: We're so pleased with Michael. He has just done so well this year. He was doing five final year subjects and he got straight 'A's' in them all. He's been accepted to do medicine – just think, a doctor in the family!

Jim: Has he. . . ?

Debbie: Yes Judy has done so well this year too – she's in Architecture at the University, you know, and the Professor of Design said that her thesis was the best he had seen in all his years teaching. We're hoping she'll get a University Medal.

Jim: Has she. . . ?

Barbara: Michael's done so well that we've promised him a car to make it easier for him to get to College – the bus service from our area is so irregular but we didn't want him to move into the University Hall – we would miss him so much if he wasn't around.

Debbie: Judy won't be around much either for the next few months. We've paid for a trip to Italy – for her to look at Italian architecture and to really have a good rest before she starts work.

Jim: Where in Italy. . . ?

Barbara: Michael went to Italy with the school this year during summer. He had a marvellous time . . .

And so the conversation went on. Poor Jim, I thought, at least he is listening and trying to engage in sequential conversation. Barbara and Debbie continued on with their 'parallel' conversation, neither one at all interested in what the other was saying. 'Ships that pass in the night', I mused to myself.

Last week I was dining with a client in the company canteen. John and I selected our meal from the cafeteria and then sat at one of the long tables next to Doreen, who had just joined the office staff. The conversation proceeded as follows –

John: Hello, you've just started in the office, haven't you. What's your name?
Doreen: Doreen.
John: When did you start?
Doreen: Yesterday.
John: Where did you come from?
Doreen: Purchasing.
John: Who did you work for there?
Doreen: Mr Hammond.
John: Ah, yes a nice chap. Who are you working for in our office?
Doreen: Mr Green.
John: Oh Jimmy! Well you should get on all right with him. Do you think you will enjoy the work?
Doreen: I hope so.

Doreen then left the table and John turned to me and said, 'She's an attractive lass but a bit quiet, don't you think. I could hardly get a word out of her'.

'Well here's a client who needs my help', I said to myself as I proceeded to outline some of the advantages that a knowledge of psychoverbal communication could bring. 'Six specific enquiries in a row – I haven't heard that many for a while', I reflected.

My children are at an age when they are entering high school, so recently my wife and I decided to buy a set of encyclopaedias which would help them in their various school projects. We telephoned one of the leading encyclopaedia companies and a representative came out to tell us about the range it offered. He arrived while I was getting some groceries out of the car. The conversation proceeded as follows –

Salesman: That's a nice car. New, is it?
Me: Yes, bought it last week.
Salesman: What attracted you to that model?
Me: Well we've got four children and there's not too many cars around these days that can comfortably seat six. I went to a couple of

dealers, looked at the other two competitors and then chose this one – it matches the house nicely, doesn't it?

We then went inside and spent some time looking at the set of encyclopaedias that he was offering. Inside, part of the conversation went as follows –

Salesman: These are beautifully printed and bound, aren't they?
Me: They sure are – I just love the feel of that shiny paper.
Salesman: Can't you just see how helpful they'll be to your children with their studies.
Me: They certainly look good.
Salesman: These are the biggest selling set of encyclopaedias in the age range 13 to 18. We've specifically aimed at this market as this is probably the time when encyclopaedias are most used. Most adults don't use encyclopaedias – they get them for their children so it makes sense to tailor the contents particularly to their needs, doesn't it?
Me: I guess so.

The conversation continued on in a similar pattern and I ultimately bought the set. 'Here', I thought, 'is someone who knows how to match his conversational style to that of his client. Must have been well trained or perhaps he has that intuitive ability to understand his customer.'

Over the years many of my clients have been in the computer industry. Two people that I remember well are Geoff Larkin and Vic Hawley. Geoff was the Sales Manager in a microcomputer retail business and Vic Hawley was the General Manager. Geoff Larkin had been with the firm about 6 months when he 'popped in' to see his boss. The following dialogue ensued –

Larkin: Have you got a minute? It's about a new idea I've got.
Hawley: Well not really, I'm very busy. Can't you send me a memo?
Larkin: It won't take long.
Hawley: Oh, I suppose so but just a minute!
Larkin: I've got a great idea of how we can increase our sales. You know the new high resolution dot matrix printer we are marketing. Well I reckon we could use it to make photocopies of drawings and pictures.
Hawley: Not another one of your bright ideas!
Larkin: We would have to design a simple light detector which could scan a page line by line and store the information digitally. We could then write a program to print out the data. Think how great it would be for facsimile transmission over the telephone. It would be ideal for screened pictures because they are just made up of dots.

Hawley: How much will it cost?

Larkin: Everyone has a microcomputer these days but Telecom facsimile transmitters are expensive. Customers would just have to buy some software and a cheap light detector unit say the size of a sheet of foolscap.

Hawley: I mean how much will it cost us to develop?

Larkin: Oh, I don't know but it wouldn't be much.

Hawley: Look, that's the trouble with you, Geoff; this is the third 'bright idea' you've told me about since you started. I'm not really interested. We're in a highly competitive business and quite frankly it's hard work maintaining our market share. New computer shops are opening up almost weekly. Our prime concern must be to hang on to what we've got. We must keep a really close eye on all costs and monitor every single lead we have.

Larkin: Yes but . . .

Hawley: And while you're here I'm not happy about the records you're keeping. I want to see a list every day of all the incoming telephone leads we get and also a list of every person that each salesman sees during the day. Each entry should be annotated with suitable comments and a space left to record 'follow-up' details. Your team is far too slack, you need to tighten up all round.

Larkin: Look, if we did that, we would have no time to develop any new leads. Haven't I increased sales by 10 per cent in the first few months I've been here. I haven't done that by sitting down and filling in a lot of bloody forms. I'm out of the office most days meeting all sorts of potential clients. In fact, it was one of them that gave me the idea for the facsimile transmitter. I know it would work really well.

Hawley: Don't get off the subject. I want to see a detailed list by the end of next week. See my secretary and make an appointment.

And so I could continue on with examples of dialogues at home, at work, at the pub, in meetings, and with friends, for I spend much of my time listening to people and the way they go about communicating. Very, very few people communicate well and it is this inability to exchange information that is at the heart of family, business and world problems. Yet it could all be so easily avoided if people understood the basic fundamental steps of what to do and what not to do when communicating with others. By the time you finish reading this book, I hope you will understand some of the 'Dos' and 'Don'ts' and be well on the way to becoming a successful communicator.

An American psychologist once said, 'Conversation in the States today is a competitive exercise where the first person to draw breath is declared the listener!' Barbara and Debbie are a bit like this. Being extroverted Thruster-Organizers (see Chapter 2), they do like talking and pushing home their point. Whilst this can be advantageous in many circumstances, it is undoubtedly 'high-risk' communication and can quickly lead to confrontationist situations.

John is a reliable, steady production manager in a manufacturing company and relies very much on direct factual communication. He is a 'pillar of strength' at work, being effective and efficient and someone you can count on to finish a job. However, his 'interrogative' enquiry style can often be very off-putting to others. In the conversation with Doreen he phrases his sentences in such a way that Doreen has little option but to answer in single phrases or short sentences.

I did admire the encyclopaedia salesman, for he knew that the key to success in communication is understanding the person you are talking to. His opening conversation about the car was a good way of finding out what sort of person I was and the basis on which I had made decisions about buying a new car. He was then able to frame his selling approach so that it matched my buying pattern. He knew that I was a visual person who always liked to see 'the big picture' and that I would get bogged down if there were too many details. He had also mastered several of the persuasion techniques that are discussed in Chapter 8.

The conversation between Geoff Larkin and Vic Hawley is similar to conversations I hear all the time in business. They are two entirely different personalities with different ways of doing things. They have what is called 'opposite models of reality' and neither understands what motivates and drives the other. Therefore their conversation is pitched all the time in terms of their own model and not that of the other person. If only they understood that people are different, they might be able to use these differences to advantage.

The problem then is that many people do not take the time to think about the person to whom they are talking. Too often they act as if they are talking to a clone of themselves and, as this is rarely the case, it is no wonder that few people are able to establish rapport and develop mutually satisfactory conversational outcomes. To be a good communicator you must accept that *people are different* and that your way of doing things, your ideas, your values are not necessarily 'absolute'. The world is full of differences and it is this diversity that has ensured the success of mankind. If you accept this and make some effort to 'climb inside the other person's model of the world' and understand him, successful communication will ensue.

In order to do this you must of course have a method of characterizing these 'people-differences' and learn to develop 'flexibility' in your interaction techniques so that you can 'lock on to the other person's natural frequency'. In my work I have successfully used the Team Management Wheel as a basis for understanding 'differences' and the Psychoverbal Communication Model as a way of teaching others how to vary their communication patterns so as to achieve their goals, whilst generating and maintaining rapport with the other person. If you follow these techniques closely and incorporate them in your day-to-day interactions, you will become, in a very short time, an effective and influential communicator at home and at work.

2
How do you like to work?

The key to successful communication is to realize that people like to work in different ways and to take account of these differences when interacting with others. One way of doing this is to understand the concepts of the Team Management Wheel – a model originally developed by myself and Charles Margerison for use with management teams (Margerison and McCann 1984, 1985; Margerison, McCann and Davies, 1988).

In our work with managers we were intrigued by the different approaches to work shown by various people and looked for a simple way of characterizing work preferences. In doing this we were guided by the writings of Carl Jung (1923), who over 60 years ago suggested several key factors which might explain why people behave in different ways.

In the workplace then we identified four key issues which are at the heart of different managerial styles and looked for a way of bringing these issues together in a readily usable model. The issues identified were –

How people prefer to relate with others.
How people prefer to gather and use information.
How people prefer to make decisions.
How people prefer to organize themselves and others.

Each day at work managers have to relate with others in order to get the work done. Some people do this in an extroverted way, meeting frequently with others, talking through ideas and enjoying a variety of tasks and activities. Other people, however, are more introverted, preferring to think things through on their own before speaking and generally not having a high need to be with others.

In the process of relating with others managers will gather and use various types of information. They will either do this in a practical or creative manner. Practical people will prefer to work with tested ideas and pay attention to the facts and details, whereas creative information gatherers are future-oriented, enjoy ambiguous situations and are always looking at the possibilities and implications.

Once the information has been gathered, it is necessary to make decisions. Some people go about this in an analytical way, setting up objective decision criteria and choosing that solution which maximizes the pay-off. Others will tend to make decisions more according to their beliefs, where personal principles and values will have a much greater impact upon their decision-making.

Decisions have to be implemented within an organizational framework and there are two distinct preferences that managers exhibit here. Some like a structured environment where things are neat and tidy and action is quickly taken to resolve issues. Others prefer to be more flexible and to make sure that all possible information has been gathered before decisions are taken. They prefer to spend their time diagnosing the situation and will tend to put off 'concluding' and 'resolving' until they have gathered all the information they can. See Figure 1.

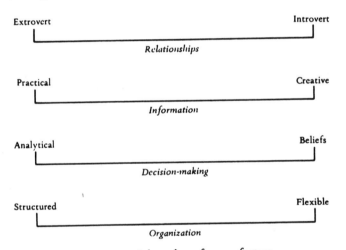

Extrovert   Introvert

Relationships

Practical   Creative

Information

Analytical   Beliefs

Decision-making

Structured   Flexible

Organization

Figure 1 *Key managerial work preference factors*

We devised a sixty-item instrument – the Team Management Index (Margerison and McCann, 1984) – to measure these four key preference factors. For each factor the index locates a position somewhere along the continua depicted in Figure 1. When the factors are combined, they create a number of interactions which describe behavioural characteristics of people in key managerial situations – characteristics such as leadership, interpersonal skills, decision-making skills and the like.

The feedback from the index is a 4000-word personal report which managers world-wide have found extremely valuable in helping them understand themselves and the people they work with. A number of organizations throughout the world now offer a Team Management profiling service based on the Index, and details are given at the end of the book.

The Team Management Wheel

To help managers understand how the four key preference factors interrelate to produce characteristic work patterns we developed the concept of the Team Management Wheel, which provides a visual representation of key differences between people. A number of team roles were identified and these describe the types of work that people prefer and also the way they go about doing that work. See Figure 2.

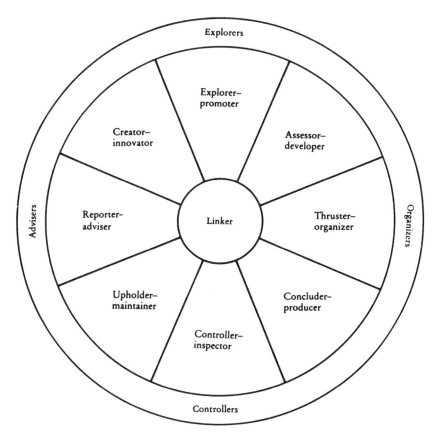

Figure 2 *The Team Management Wheel*

A person's score from the Team Management Index can be mapped on to the wheel, and generally the result is a major preference for one of the team roles indicated and two related roles as 'back-ups'. For example, someone might have a major preference to be a creator–innovator with related or 'back-up' roles as thruster–organizer and concluder–producer.

The wheel has eight sectors and these are related to the various combinations arising from the four key work preference factors indicated in Figure 2. For example, the category of explorer–promoter results because of a particular interaction between the extrovert and creative dimensions, which gives people a preference for promoting and selling new ideas and concepts and generally being entrepreneurial. The concluder–producer sector fits those people who score strongly on the practical and structured dimensions. This results in these people exhibiting a 'concluding' behaviour in many of their activities. They value effectiveness and efficiency and can usually be counted on to carry a job through to completion.

The north–south axis of the wheel indicates a behavioural axis which describes activities as exploring or controlling. In short, people can prefer work which has a strong element of control or a job where there is a high degree of exploring and looking for new opportunities. Some people prefer both exploring and controlling but usually we have found people to have more of a preference one way or the other: maybe 60–40 in one direction or 70–30 in the other.

The east–west axis describes the work content as being either organizing or advising. We found that people prefer to be in either advisory work or in a job where they can exercise their organizing interests and abilities. Again some people prefer both and can do both equally well, but in general most people lean one way or the other.

A knowledge of a person's location on the Team Management Wheel can help you enormously in your interpersonal dealings. By understanding what motivates these people and how they prefer to work you can develop interaction strategies that can help prevent potential conflicts. These strategies are examined in the next chapter. For now, though, it is important that you understand the major characteristics of each sector on the Wheel and learn to recognize these in other people.

Creator–innovators

Creator–innovators are people who are very much 'future-oriented' and will enjoy thinking up new ideas and new ways of doing things. Usually they are very independent and will pursue their ideas regardless of present systems and methods. They therefore need to be managed in such a way that their ideas can be developed without too many organizational constraints. Sometimes organizations set up research and development units (often separated from the production units) to allow these people to experiment with their ideas.

Creator–innovators are sometimes accused (usually by opposites on the wheel) of 'having their head in the clouds', but this is usually because they are looking to tomorrow rather than worrying about today. They are usually not very structured in the way they go about things and may sometimes appear disorganized and absent-minded. Early in my career I remember working with Matthew Reece, who was a creator–innovator *par excellence*. He was responsible for some major inventions in the company but most managers had difficulty in working with him as he kept unusual hours and insisted on 'being his own boss'. One day Matthew came down to the car park ready to go home and discovered that his car had been stolen during the day. He contacted the security guard, who rang the police and both of them were waiting at the front gate when Matthew's wife arrived in the car to pick him up from work. Matthew was so engrossed in his problems that he forgot he had travelled to work by train that day and left the car with his wife to take it to be serviced!

Some creator–innovators are quite introverted, preferring to be 'back-room' people working on their own or in small groups on important problems. Others can be more outgoing and even zealous in the way they put forward their ideas. Another creator–innovator I used to work with was called 'The Preacher' because of the enthusiasm he showed for each new idea and the way he would put foward his views. We could all imagine him standing at the pulpit delivering a powerful sermon to the congregation.

Explorer–promoters

Explorer–promoters are excellent at taking ideas and promoting them to others, both inside and outside the organization. They enjoy being with people and will usually have a network of people that they use when gathering information and testing out opportunities. Usually they are advocates of change and are highly energized, active people who often have several different activities on the go at once. They enjoy being 'out and about' and are good at bringing back contacts, information and resources which can help the organization move forward.

Explorer–promoters are entrepreneurial risk-takers who can be very persuasive. They are often influential and can talk easily, even on subjects where they are not experts. They are excellent at seeing the 'big picture' and developing an enthusiasm for an innovation amongst other people. However, they are not always interested in 'controlling' and 'organizing' and do not always pay sufficient attention to details. In this regard they often benefit from having a concluder–producer or controller–inspector to work with, although they may sometimes have difficulties in interacting with these people.

Explorer–promoters enjoy 'off-the-cuff' conversations and need to interact with others to be at their productive best. It is not for them to sit in a back-room working alone on their problems – they need people to stimulate them. In this regard they can be energy-draining, almost sucking out energy from people around them.

Many explorer-promoters I know have 'elastic egos'. They are quick to see an opportunity and seize it before it disappears. Sooner or later in their careers they get their fingers burnt but it doesn't seem to worry them – they rebound back again, looking for the next opportunity. It is this characteristic of course that makes for a successful entrepreneur.

Assessor–developers

Assessor–developers are located on the Wheel mid-way between explorers and organizers and therefore exhibit both of these types' characteristics. They may not always think up good ideas for themselves but they are excellent at taking the idea and making it work in practice. They are usually sociable, outgoing people who enjoy looking for new markets or opportunities. They will then take the idea and match it to the opportunity, always mindful of the organizational 'bottom line' constraints. They often make good product development managers or people concerned with assessing new ventures.

Assessor–developers usually display a strong analytical approach and are at their best with several different possibilities to analyse and develop before a decision is made. They like organizing new activities and respond well to such challenges, taking an idea and pushing it forward into a workable scheme. However, once the activity has been set up and been shown to work, they will often lose interest, preferring to move on to the next project rather than engage in the production and control of the output.

Thruster–organizers

In my earlier career as an engineer I worked with many people who would 'map' into the thruster-organizer sector of the Team Management Wheel. They were chosen for a job because of their ability to make things happen. One person I remember well was Dan Crocker.

Dan was a Project Manager on a civil engineering contract and he believed in setting objectives and working to a plan based wherever possible on his past experiences and the well-tested procedures which he had developed on past assignments. He was definitely action-oriented and had the ability to deliver projects on time and to budget.

Dan was an outgoing person who enjoyed meeting his staff to discuss issues. He enjoyed the excitement of a 'crisis' and hated things to be in disarray. His meetings with the site agent and engineering staff were often fiery, as Dan would not take 'no' for an answer. When obstacles were put in his way, he quickly became annoyed and would 'drive' endlessly until opposition was worn away.

Despite his practical approach and desire for action, Dan was highly analytical. He kept detailed costs on all parts of his project and had set up quite a sophisticated computer model which could do a simple cost/benefit analysis for him. He was a formidable 'arguer' and a definite conflict-confronter.

In earlier years when Dan had been a site agent himself he had sometimes unconsciously caused union problems. He was often seen as impatient and 'pushy' and would consider emotional matters such as people's feelings as secondary to getting the work done. He had no compunction about sacking people and this had been the cause of a major strike some years back. His biggest problem was his tendency to act first and think later, although since becoming project manager he had attempted to control himself and would often 'count to ten' before responding to issues which irritated him.

Dan's behaviour is a perfect example of the extroverted thruster–organizer who will push on to get results regardless of opposition. There is also another type of thruster–organizer who goes about his work in a quieter way, sometimes keeping his ideas to himself until he is sure of a particular course of action. He will then leap into action, demanding results from those working with him. Both types, though, are excellent at organizing people and systems to ensure that deadlines can be met. They will set objectives, establish plans, work out who should do what and then press for action. They tend to be task-oriented and in their pursuit of goals may sometimes ignore people's feelings. This more than anything else gets them into trouble with their peers and subordinates.

Concluder–producers

Concluder–producers are strongly practical people who can be counted on to carry things through to the end. Their strength is in setting up plans and standard systems so that output can be achieved on a regular basis in a controlled and orderly fashion. For this reason they usually do not like rapid change, as it interferes with the efficient systems they have established for doing the work. This may sometimes cause them difficulties with creator–innovators and explorer–promoters who continually try to change the way of doing things.

For concluder–producers the challenge lies not in dreaming up new ideas but in doing the work effectively and efficiently. Therefore they are often more patient than others with routine work, as the drive for them comes from 'a job well done'. As a result, they are sought after as managers for their ability to work in a quick, reliable, dependable and stable manner and deliver results.

Our studies with managers (Margerison, McCann and Davies, 1988) have shown that concluder–producers are in demand as managers – some 27 per cent of a world-wide sample of middle and senior managers had the concluder–producer role as their major preference. Most of these tended to have a preference for being introverted rather than extroverted. This result is not surprising, as the demands of many organizations match well with the concluder–producer preference. When concluder–producers join an organization, they do their job without fuss, they deliver to a deadline, they carry things through to the end, and they are stable and resilient in crises. All these attributes make them stand out as 'just the sort of person we need in this organization'. They therefore rise quickly to the middle ranks and become organizational 'Rocks of Gibraltar'.

Controller–inspectors

Controller–inspectors are quiet, reflective people who enjoy the detailed side of work and like working with facts and figures. They are usually careful and meticulous and can spend long periods of time on a particular task working quietly on their own. This stands in direct opposition to explorer–promoters, who need a wide variety of tasks to engage their attention and people around with whom they can interact.

Controller–inspectors are comfortable working within the rules and regulations which have been established by others. They would argue that the rules have been made to ensure that the organization works in the most efficient manner and therefore everyone should obey them. For this reason they enjoy working in situations where their output is guided by organizational or governmental regulations. We have found many of them working in finance, accounting and quality-control positions, where their 'inspecting' preferences are important assets for the work they are doing.

Although controller–inspectors may not talk a great deal in meetings, when they do, it is important to listen to them. They like to think things through before speaking and therefore when they decide to comment, they are usually succinct, accurate and to the point, unlike more extroverted people who enjoy talking through their unformed ideas.

Upholder–maintainers

Upholder–maintainers are people with strong personal values and principles, and these are of prime importance in their decision-making. Usually they have a high concern for people and will be strongly supportive of those who share the same ideals and values as they do.

Earlier in my career I remember working with Tessa Wilson, who was a Personnel Officer in a multinational oil and chemical company. She had very firm beliefs about life and spent much of her time outside work engaged in community activities. She ran the Sunday School at the local church and was an 'Akela' in the cub pack.

Tessa was very loyal to the oragnization and had a strong sense of duty. She had very high standards of propriety and expected it in others. To her, harmony and good relationships were most important and she always tried to develop a spirit of cooperation rather than confrontation. Tessa had a reputation for supporting people who felt they had been unfairly treated by the company. Although she was quiet and reserved and on occasions even self-effacing, she had an ability to listen and be sympathetic. On many occasions she had taken people's cases right to the top, and would not give in until she felt that justice had been done. Few people were able to shift her on matters of conscience.

Tessa enjoyed her job, as she felt the personnel team was close and supportive of one another. She disliked being rushed, as this affected her high quality standards. She had left her previous job in advertising, as she found it difficult to cope with the long hours. She felt the job interfered with what she called her 'quality of life'.

Tessa's characteristics are typical of many upholder–maintainers I have met in organizations. They prefer to work in a control-oriented supportive way, making sure that things are done according to their standards. In addition, they prefer an advisory role in the background rather than a leading executive role. However, because of their strong principles, they will 'dig their heels in' when confronting issues which oppose their beliefs. They will not react in an extroverted, quick-tempered way but more in a resilient, obstinate manner which can sometimes be very irritating to thruster–organizers. In fact a meeting between a thruster–organizer and an upholder–maintainer will some-times be like the irresistible force meeting the immovable object!

Reporter–advisers

Reporter–advisers represent the classic advisory role on the Team Management Wheel. They are excellent at gathering information and putting it together in such a way as can be readily understood. If they are more introverted, they will probably rely on written formats for their information, whereas if they are more extroverted, they will be good communicators and probably rely on a network of colleagues and acquaintances for their data.

Reporter–advisers are patient people who prefer to make sure they have all the information before they take action. This often causes others, particularly thruster–organizers, to accuse them of procrastination, but reporter–advisers will typically respond, 'How can I take action unless I have all the information?' Thruster–organizers, who often take action with only 20 per cent of the available information, sometimes find this hard to understand.

Some years ago I was a consultant to a timber company and one of their staff was a good 'role-model' of a reporter–adviser. He was the logging manager – let's call him Sam.

The company was having some problems and the factory manager was asked to leave. He decided to go 'overnight' and this left the company with the task of finding a replacement quickly. They decided to take their time so that they would get the 'right' man and therefore asked the logging manager to become Acting Factory Manager in the interim.

The morale of the senior management team was understandably low but Sam was well liked and he threw himself into the job. At the end of 3 months the factory was in much better shape and Sam, with his low key supportive approach, had succeeded in getting the team 'back on the tracks'. The senior management thought he had done such a good job that it offered him the job permanently.

During a counselling session with Sam I discovered that he disliked many of the aspects of his new job and was unsure as to whether he should take on the manager's role permanently. He found the job quite stressful and particularly hated having to make quick decisions, which in many cases were necessary as they affected the production line. He felt he was under considerable stress and found it difficult to sleep. His wife had recently accused him of becoming 'impossible to live with' since he had taken on the manager's role. Sam in fact was working in a job which demanded many of the characteristics of a thruster–organizer approach, but on the Team Management Wheel a thruster–organizer is as far away from the reporter–adviser as one can get.

Sam began to long for his old job as the logging manager, where he had a dependable team of loggers and supervisors. He enjoyed his job there and had made it into one with the prime responsibility of travelling around the forests selecting those trees and thinnings for the next 3 months' felling. This gave him a chance to gather a lot of data about the state of the forests and he even had 'pet' names for some of the larger trees: After much soul-searching Sam decided to go back to his logging job, and when I saw him recently he said that he had never regretted his decision.

Linking

In the middle of the team management wheel is the area of the Linker. All managers of teams need to develop the skills of linking, which are designed to bond together the different roles into a high performing team. Linking is different to the team roles which are depicted as segments of the wheel, as it is not a preference but a set of skills that all managers need to learn.

Basically there are three general aspects to linking – internal linking, external linking and informal linking.

People who are effective at internal linking are very good at integrating and producing working arrangements amongst people. They will ensure that the team members are kept up-to-date on important issues and that there is a high degree of team cohesiveness and cooperation. They are excellent at allocating work and usually set high standards and examples for others to follow. They are readily available when problems arise and will act to ensure that these are resolved effectively and efficiently.

Managers who are good external linkers are in many ways good 'Foreign Secretaries'. They represent their team well in negotiations at high levels and ensure that adequate resources are obtained to do the job at hand. They also open up communication channels with other groups working at the same level and will defend their teams against external criticism. They have usually identified those external links which need to be strengthened and developed ways to do this. Someone described as a good 'organizational politician' is often a good external linker.

Above and beyond this there is informal linking, where people actually do facilitate interactions between individuals and across departments to ensure work is done more effectively. Many people who are good at informal linking do not have a formal role as a manager or leader but do it because of the way in which they do their job effectively. For example, many secretaries have developed excellent linking skills and act as a coordinating point for members working in teams, particularly where the leader has concentrated on external linking at the expense of internal linking.

All these three areas of linking demand excellence in communication, and in this sense this book is all about developing the most important linking skill – that of communicating with others. In another book (Margerison and McCann, 1990) the management issues of linking are discussed in more detail.

Team role distributions

It is interesting to look at some of the data from the Team Management Index on a population of managers from the United Kingdom, the United States of America, Canada, Australia, New Zealand and South East Asia. Davies (1988) reports a breakdown of team management roles for a sample of 3738 managers. The data are shown in Table 1.

Table 1   *Distribution of team roles*

Team role	Proportion (%)
Creator–innovator	9.2
Explorer–promoter	8.7
Assessor–developer	17.5
Thruster–organizer	26.5
Concluder–producer	26.7
Controller–inspector	7.5
Upholder–maintainer	1.9
Reporter–adviser	2.1

71 per cent of the sample falls on the right-hand side of the wheel in the three sectors of assessor–developer, thruster–organizer, and concluder–producer. These sectors have a common characteristic in a preference for organizing, and it is not surprising that managers with such a preference have gravitated to positions of influence in the organizations sampled. However, you will see in the later chapters, particularly in Chapter 7 on Leading, that these people do not always have a natural ability to listen, and their general weakness in communication is responsible for a lot of them failing to achieve truly high-performance in the way they manage their teams.

How to determine team roles

The team management wheel is the 'underpinning cog' for much of what follows, and therefore it is important to characterize people as closely as possible into segments of the Wheel, for it will enable you to employ communication strategies which will increase your chances of a successful interaction. The best way of doing this is to use the team management index and receive a 4000-word assessment on the person with whom you communicate regularly (see p. 127 for details). Whilst this can be readily done for your colleagues and subordinates and even your bosses, it may not be practical to do it for customers and clients. For these situations it is possible to get some idea of their position on the Wheel by using the checklist given in the tables below. This will not give you any information on the related roles but it may enable you to assign a person to a particular quadrant on the Wheel.

To use the tables, think of the person you are trying to categorize and tick those words which apply to him. Go through all the words and then add up the ticks in each category. The team role with the most ticks will give you some idea of the likely location on the Wheel. However, the assessment is only very approximate, and suffers also from the weakness that it is your perception of the other person and not his perception of himself. We have found many times that there is a potential here for misinterpretation of a person's major team role. To be sure of your assessment it is worth getting your colleagues to complete the Team Management Index and have it processed. It takes about 10 minutes to answer the sixty questions.

Explorer–promoters
Outgoing
Enthusiastic
Warm
Talkative
Stimulating
Imaginative
Impulsive
Excitable
Persuasive
Opinionated
Emotional
Far-sighted
Dramatic
Risk-taker

Assessor–developers
Outgoing
Analytical
Experimenter
Idea-developer
Challenge-seeker
Sociable
Organizer
Pragmatic
Logical
Planner
Product-champion
Talkative
Group-worker
Expressive

Thruster–organizers
Determined
Action-oriented
Disciplined
Tough
Independent
Logical
Decisive
Factual
Commanding
Impatient
Task-oriented
Stubborn
Competitive
Conflict-confronter

Concluder–producers
Steady
Reliable
Effective
Efficient
Dependable
Finisher
Organized
Systematic
Orderly
Practical
Deadline-conscious
Crisis-hardy
Change-resistant
Present-oriented

Controller–inspector
Conservative
Quiet
Practical
Logical

Upholder–maintainer
Beliefs-based
Quiet
Supportive
'Defender-of-the-faith'

Detail-oriented
Thorough
Accurate
Conscientious
Dependable
Reserved
Critical
Distant
'Nit-picker'

Reporter–advisers
Helpful
Kind
Well-liked
Thoughtful
Knowledgeable
Supportive
Tolerant
Easy-going
Information-gatherer
Willing
Cooperative
Soft
Conflict-avoiding
Procrastinating
Principled

Conscientious
Traditional
Reserved
'Long fuse'
Conflict-avoiding
Controlling
Advising
Consensus-seeking
Self-effacing

Creator–innovators
Imaginative
Intuitive
Independent
'Head-in-the-clouds'
Researcher
Innovator
Information-seeker
Procrastinating
Absent-minded
Non-finisher
Deadline-misser
Future-oriented
Flexible
Idea-generator
Visionary

3

Plan your conversation with strategic pacing

We all live in a world containing thousands of different people and objects – the so-called 'real world'. Yet we do not operate directly on that real world but create our own model through perceptions developed by our senses of sight, sound, feeling, taste and smell. It is through this model that we value and assess our interactions with the world.

People are different. The differences are largely due to the different model they develop as they go through life. These differences are highlighted in the Team Management Wheel, where those with role preferences in opposite parts of the wheel will have a different model of the world.

When we interact with others, we translate our model of the world into words and use these to attain our outcomes. These words and the supporting communication aids (tone, tempo, body positions) very much reflect our own views of the world. Therefore when people from different parts of the Team Management Wheel interact, there is potential for conflict to arise as different models of the world are interacting. When opposites come together, there is a great potential for things to go wrong and the discussion or conversation may well be 'doomed' before the first word has been uttered.

One of the goals in teamwork is to influence others so that group outcomes may be attained. On one-to-one encounters the goal may well be to conduct the conversation in such a way that you succeed in obtaining your immediate needs. To do this it is necessary to have flexibility in your interpersonal approaches and adopt the technique of pacing.

Pacing is a technique for temporarily modifying your model of the world so that it matches the other person's. This matching shows the other person that you understand 'where they are coming from'. Unless you take time to establish 'a pace' early in the conversation, the chances of a successful interaction occurring are markedly reduced.

There are two types of pacing – 'strategic pacing' and 'operational pacing'. Strategic pacing involves setting a strategy for the way you intend to structure an impending conversation, using all the knowledge you have about the other person's model of the world. Operational pacing, discussed in the next chapter, is the technique to use when the conversation is actually in progress.

Strategic pacing

The Team Management Wheel is an ideal model to use to formulate your pacing strategy. An understanding of how people approach their job can help you present your ideas in a way that is acceptable to them. To do this it is particularly important to look for the positive qualities in people rather than concentrate on the negative aspects. We all find it easier to be negative than positive and constructive. Explorer–promoters, for example, often see controller–inspectors as boring, pendantic, over-critical, 'nit-picking', 'i-dotters and t-crossers', whereas controller–inspectors, in turn, will accuse explorer–promoters of being wafflers, loud, brash, arrogant, insincere, and even having 'a tenuous grasp of the facts'. If we focus on negatives, the chances of having worthwhile and meaningful dialogues are very much reduced.

The conversation between Geoff Larkin and Vic Hawley in Chapter 1 (page 3) is a good example of a negative conversation between two people. Geoff Larkin is an enthusiastic, outgoing person who is stimulated by the challenge of a new idea. He has many of the characteristics of an explorer–promoter. His boss Vic Hawley is a quieter, more reserved person who is very analytical in his approach and probably quite resistant to change. He has many of the characteristics of a controller–inspector.

Both parties have failed to use strategic pacing to help them get across their point. Larkin should have perhaps known that Hawley didn't like being interrupted without an appointment and that he probably preferred to communicate in written form. Likewise Hawley should have appreciated that Larkin needed to talk his idea through with someone. If Hawley was too busy, he could have arranged a suitable time for discussion or perhaps have suggested that Larkin talked to someone who could help him with facts and figures – maybe an assessor–developer or a concluder–producer.

In his responses Hawley makes use of several negatives which should have been clues to Larkin that perhaps now was not the right time to present information to his boss. Of course it would be difficult for Larkin to 'hold his tongue', for explorer–promoters like to have someone to talk to as it helps them get their ideas straight. Nonetheless both parties should have appreciated the different 'models of reality' that they have and used strategic pacing.

Strategic pacing is a vital concept to use in important negotiations and discussions. It is also very useful in 'managing upwards', where the way you present yourself and your ideas can have an important influence on the outcome of any discussions. To assist with formulating various pacing strategies, some of the key points for each sector of the Team Management Wheel are listed below.

Pacing the explorer–promoter
Explorer–promoters tend to present themselves to the world as outgoing, enthusiastic, warm, talkative, stimulating, imaginative, impulsive, excitable, far-sighted, and persuasive. They are also often seen as opinionated, emotional, competitive, dramatic, intuitive and thought-provoking.

Explorer–promoters are highly motivated by ideas and the possibility of future benefits. Therefore a rapport can immediately be established by exploring together new ideas and possible solutions. You should not rush explorer–promoters into a decision but give them time to talk through all their ideas. Explorer–promoters enjoy 'positive stroking' and like to feel their ideas are appreciated. Therefore it is often a good plan to let the explorer–promoter take the credit for any ideas that are deve·oped.

Explorer–promoters have a natural tendency to 'get off the subject' as one idea will often spawn another and so on. In these situations get the explorer–promoter 'back on track' by using a lead phrase such as 'That's a really good idea, how do you think we could use it in this situation?'

Explorer–promoters are often opinionated and have a need to be recognized for their innovative contribution. You should avoid arguing with explorer–promoters unless you feel it is absolutely necessary. A better strategy is to steer the explorer–promoter away from the current idea or solution and look for new areas that you can both share with excitement. It is usually fairly easy to change the topic of conversation with explorer–promoters by throwing in a new, potentially stimulating idea or thought.

Explorer–promoters do not always enjoy criticism and you should allow them to have the 'limelight' if at all possible. They usually form opinions fairly readily and you should look to the ones you agree with rather then taking issue with those you disagree with. Explorer-promoters often change their opinion readily and there is little point in taking issue with particular opinions which in the course of time will probably change anyway.

For explorer–promoters the challenge and excitement resides in formulating the idea and talking it through. They often show little interest in how these ideas and objectives might be reached and usually don't want to be involved in the details, or when they do, they may well get them wrong. Therefore at particular points in the discussion you should use the skills of summarizing and suggest possible ways of implementing some of the ideas you have agreed upon. If you are prepared to take responsibility for organizing the details, it will be much appreciated by the explorer–promoter. Offer to write up the details agreed upon and minute any action that you both agree should be done.

Because explorer–promoters are always looking to the future and seeking opportunities, they do not always remember what they might have agreed with others. Therefore if you are wanting agreements or undertakings on particular subjects, it is a wise move to put them in writing and circulate them to the explorer–promoter. You will then have 'black and white' evidence should the agreements be questioned.

Explorer–promoters are often 'switched-off' by discussions containing excessive detail. If you want to sell something to an explorer–promoter, don't go into detail. For example, if you were selling a new car you could talk about the multi-point electronic fuel injection, the crossflow cylinder head design, the low mass short skirt pistons, the temperature-controlled fluid clutch fan and the self-diagnostic engine management system computer; however, you could be wasting your time and you might lose the sale. A better strategy might be to concentrate on 'the big picture' and explain, for example, what this car could do for the explorer–promoter. General statements like 'this car gives 33 per cent more power and uses 15 per cent less fuel than other similar models' are more likely to be positively received.

Strategic pacing is very useful in interviews. If you were being interviewed for a job by an explorer–promoter, one successful strategy might be to concentrate on all the new, exciting things you would do or introduce if you were hired for the job. An outgoing, enthusiastic style would establish immediate empathy with the interviewer. However, if you were to concentrate too much on the details of your last job, you might well appear boring to the explorer–promoter.

If you are an explorer–promoter yourself, you will automatically have good rapport with other explorer–promoters, although there will undoubtedly be competition when differing ideas are proposed. There may well be a temptation to proceed on the basis of a warm feeling that somehow or other everything will work out satisfactorily. You should force youself to concentrate on the specifics and be sure all parties are clear on who is doing what. There is a natural tendency for explorer–promoters to bite off more than they can chew and you need to assure yourself that both parties will be able to fulfil their undertakings in the time available.

In summary, explorer–promoters respond well to discussions about future goals, ideas and people rather than deliberations in terms of cold, factual present-day realities. Therefore in your initial dealings you should allow the conversation to concentrate on the future, and only when you have established rapport should you attempt to focus on present-day realities.

Pacing the controller–inspector

Controller-inspectors tend to present themselves to the world as conservative, quiet, practical, logical, detail-oriented, thorough, con-scientious, dependable and accurate. They are also often seen as austere, reserved, distant, and over-critical.

Controller–inspectors are 'down-to-earth' practical people who will immediately respect others who show understanding of their principles and thoughtful approach. You will need to demonstrate to them that you can 'act' rather than 'talk' and that you really can make a specific, well organized contribution to the current project or topic under discussion. Controller–inspectors will particularly appreciate written contributions, as they enable them to reflect and consider the issues.

Controller–inspectors are highly critical of people who oversell themselves, and explorer–promoters in particular need to temper their approach here. Commit yourself only to what you know you can do and don't be over-optimistic. Try to point out the disadvantages as well as the advantages in any plans or discussions.

You should not rush controller–inspectors but give them time to consider the issues, particularly if you are proposing new ways of doing things. Controller–inspectors move with 'deliberateness', and you should slow down the pace and develop 'low key' persistence. Time spent at the early stages of an interaction with controller–inspectors is recovered with interest later, because once a commitment is gained, controller–inspectors usually stand by it.

Controller–inspectors like to feel that their point of view is fully understood by others. If you are having difficulty with them, ask yourself whether you have listened to their views and shown you understand, even if they disagree with yours. Take time to explain your position in a well thought out, organized, systematic way. A written report is often helpful here.

Controller–inspectors do not always make themselves as available as others on the Team Management Wheel. In general they don't appreciate people 'popping in' with new proposals or ideas they want to talk about. A controller–inspector likes to be prepared, and therefore you should signal your forthcoming discussion by sending a memo outlining the points, and, if possible, enclosing a written report. As a general rule avoid 'surprises' with controller–inspectors, and prepare them in advance by way of written memos.

Controller–inspectors often talk more slowly than others, carefully thinking out words before they utter them. Therefore you should breathe slowly and deeply during the encounter so as to slow down your tempo and match your conversational speed and tone to theirs. Controller–inspectors appreciate people who think out the issues before they speak, and slowing down your conversational speed will enable you to do this. Fast, enthusiastic speakers tend to be viewed as 'wafflers', an aspect generally disliked by controller–inspectors.

In interviews you should concentrate on practical details. For example, in a job interview a successful strategy could be one where you explore in detail some of the aspects of your previous job and how it relates to the position you are seeking. Controller–inspectors will be less impressed if you concentrate on the future, highlighting all the exciting new things you will do if you are given the job. They will want to concentrate on the past and be convinced that you can show concrete, practical evidence that what you have done in the past fits you for this position.

It is not easy to establish rapport with controller–inspectors unless you are close to them on the Team Management Wheel. They tend to be highly critical and naturally sceptical. Therefore in new encounters with people they may well expect others to oversell themselves or overstate their case. In opening 'gambits' with the controller–inspector you should pace the conversation initially by only making statements which can be readily verified in the mind of the controller–inspector. This is often the reason why we talk about the weather or other trivial matters when we interact with people we don't know well. Unconsciously we are attempting to establish rapport by trading easily verifiable statements.

Pacing the thruster–organizer

Thruster–organizers tend to present themselves to the world as determined, action-oriented, disciplined, tough, independent, logical, decisive and commanding. They are also often seen as impatient, non-listening, stubborn, unfeeling, 'bossy' and task-oriented.

Thruster–organizers are action-oriented and like to push forward with task objectives. Personal relationships are not so important to the thruster–organizer, so you should at all times keep interactions business-like unless you sense that the thruster–organizer wants a personal relationship as part of the objective.

To establish rapport with the thruster–organizer it is often fruitful to concentrate on specific questions and statements rather than general ones. 'What' questions are particularly well received when they focus on the task issues. 'What has to be done?' or 'What has to be achieved?' are useful questions to ask the thruster–organizer. 'How' questions, which often help explorer–promoters talk through their ideas, should be minimized when dealing with thruster–organizers. They know the action they want but may not necessarily have thought it through. Therefore if you can focus on 'What' questions and look for specific areas where you can provide concrete assistance, you will get on well with them.

Thruster–organizers are usually comfortable with conflict and will often confront issues head on. If you disagree with a thruster–organizer, take issue with the facts only and avoid bringing in personal issues or attacking them personally. Explain specifically why you can't agree with their proposed actions and offer soundly based alternative solutions for consideration. If you can't agree over a particular issue, finish the discussion by summarizing your point of view. Make sure you indicate specifically how their proposed 'path' will prevent the issue from being resolved in the quickest and most effective manner. By concentrating on factual issues you can often separate out task interactions and friendship interactions.

Thruster–organizers like to be rewarded for their efforts in concrete ways, preferring material gains to, say, public recognition. Therefore they will enjoy bonuses, profit-sharing and the like.

If you want to impress a thruster–organizer, be punctual, do what you say, and make things happen. Thruster–organizers don't always enjoy being concerned with the details and they will particularly appreciate someone who can do this effectively and efficiently.

Thruster–organizers dislike ambiguity, and like to converge as quickly as possible on solutions. Sometimes, however, they may not have all the information and can make decisions based on incorrect or insufficient data. Therefore you can help thruster–organizers by making sure you are well briefed on the subject under discussion. Make sure you have 'done your homework' and gathered together all the information upon which sound decisions can be made.

If you are from the 'advising' part of the Team Management Wheel, you are likely to see 'people problems' long before thruster–organizers. Point these out to them, indicating what effect their action is having on the people concerned. Explain how these people are being affected but relate the information to task issues. For example, you might indicate that 'the decision made is an unpopular one and that several people have been upset by it. The result could well be a lack of commitment to the project and the chances of it succeeding could be significantly reduced'. You might then go on and suggest how things might be improved.

If you are a thruster–organizer yourself, you need to be careful in your dealings with other thruster–organizers. Your desire for action will be reinforced by other thruster–organizers and the probability of a hasty decision is increased. Competition is great amongst thruster–organizers, and if different views are held, there is great potential for the conversation to go 'off the rails'. Therefore you should focus on goals and get agreement in general on the desired outcomes. You should then give other thruster–organizers the freedom to deliver the agreed goals in their own way, allowing them independence and individuality.

Pacing the reporter–adviser

Reporter–advisers tend to present themselves to the world as helpful, kind, thoughtful, knowledgeable, supportive, tolerant, easy-going, willing and cooperative. They are also often seen as soft-hearted, procrastinating, conflict-avoiding and non-threatening.

Reporter–advisers have strong beliefs about work, life and people. Therefore to establish rapport with these people you need to understand their feelings and realize their desire for a personal relationship in any team projects or business undertakings in which they are participants. It may be useful for you to investigate the background of the reporter-adviser – family, hobbies, interests and the like – and pick out an area which is of interest to you. Sharing and comparing information around areas of common interest is a powerful way of establishing rapport with reporter–advisers. To them business and personal interests are inseparable, unlike the thruster–organizer, who normally manages to separate out these issues.

Cooperation is important to reporter–advisers and they make excellent team-members once they feel their contribution is appreciated. They do not usually want public recognition but do appreciate warm, personal thanks for a job well done. Above all they want harmony in working relationships, and thruster–organizers in particular need to understand this if they want to get the best out of the reporter–adviser.

Although reporter–advisers have strong beliefs, they will not always push these forward, particularly if friendships or cooperation are likely to be threatened. Therefore they may agree with your goals willingly so as to maintain the spirit of teamwork. In fact this is one of the reasons why reporter–advisers are so well liked – because they are seen as willing, helpful and supportive. Therefore you should take time to ask reporter-advisers what their specific outcomes are before you present yours. Where there are significant differences, you need to spend time matching outcomes so that the spirit of cooperation can be developed. If you do agree readily on a subject, try this statement: 'I'm glad we see eye-to-eye on this issue; we should really be able to cooperate well. Tell me, though, can you see any areas in particular where there could be some possible future disagreements?'

If you do disagree with a reporter–adviser, you need to have a special tact in presenting your opinions. You should initially avoid discussing the facts of the issue but concentrate on the reporter–adviser's opinions and feelings. Use feeling-type words in your conversation. 'How do you **feel** about the situation. . . ?'; 'How does my decision **strike** you. . . ?'; and so on. Show that you understand the other person's feelings by again using feeling-type words – 'I **appreciate** how you **feel** on this matter . . .'; 'I can understand how you might be **upset** about the situation . . .', etc. If the disagreement is major, you should expect hurt feelings from the reporter–adviser, and these could be long-lasting or interfere with productivity, if you don't take the trouble to show concern.

Reporter–advisers are information-oriented rather than action-oriented, and like to find out as much as possible about a situation before committing themselves. Therefore they do not like being pushed hard for action, particularly when they believe that more information is required. In these situations you should agree that more time and information would be desirable but point out why it is important that the decision is taken now. The general approach with reporter–advisers is –

I appreciate that you feel . . . (show your complete and sincere understanding of the problem), but let me tell you the problem I have . . . (explain why your decision disagrees with theirs).

If you are a reporter–adviser yourself, you will have automatic rapport with other reporter–advisers; however, you need to be aware of the natural tendency to make judgments on beliefs or feelings and to be easy-going. You should watch out for these tendencies, which reinforce themselves in group situations, and at least one of the reporter–advisers should become more hard-nosed, insistent or directive, so that goals are established and action plans developed.

In summary, reporter–advisers like to be treated as 'people' and they value sincerity. You should provide these people with personal assurances that you will take into account their views and opinions and not dismiss them outright. Show an interest in their personal achievements both at work and outside in the community generally.

Another example which shows the need for strategic pacing is highlighted below in the case of 'Rush Orders'.

Rush orders

In a meeting between John Ross, the Production Administrator in a manufacturing plant, and his boss, Dennis Walton, the following dialogue took place –

Ross: I like to work in a systematic, orderly way. The problem is that I never get time to do things properly.

Walton: Well we all have to make time.

Ross: That's impossible when people keep interrupting me all the time.

Walton: What do you mean?

Ross: Well you interrupt me a lot. As soon as I get down to planning out how production is going, you rush in with another urgent order. The whole place is so customer-oriented that we upset everyone just to please a few big customers.

Walton: Without those customers we would be out of a job. Your systems have got to cope with rush orders.

Ross: That just leads to crisis management with certain customers queue-jumping. It is also costly, because we have to change the machines to do these special runs.

Walton: Yes but . . .

Ross: Look, the problem is I don't get enough time to plan, and the result is we are continually behind in supplying our smaller customers. Also maintenance of machines gets overlooked because we don't have time to do it. Since the machine operators are continually changing their runs, they don't fill in the records and I can't do a proper costing. The whole thing is a shambles. I hate this ad hoc approach to management – we never finish anything the way it should be done.

Walton: John, I know you are a bit of a perfectionist but keeping the records straight is not going to get us more sales. We have to be flexible in our approach and be ready to change runs at a moment's notice.

Ross: Well I'm not coming to next Monday's management meeting.

Walton: Why?

Ross: I would have thought it was obvious. I have not had time to plan. When I do make a plan, it is changed without consulting me as soon as a big rush order comes in, and I don't have accurate cost figures as a result. Besides which, there is no point in talking when there are so many others who think they know more about how to run the place.

In this case John Ross seems to be a very orderly person who likes to work to a system. He has many of the characteristics of a concluder-producer. Dennis Walton, his boss, obviously is not aware of Ross's preference to work in this way, and his opening reply 'Well we all have to make time' is probably responsible for the outburst which comes later. Walton's 'flexible' approach is annoying to Ross, and he finds it hard to establish a good working relationship with his boss. Using strategic pacing, Walton should have indicated that he understood how important it was for factory efficiency to have all the run schedules planned in advance but then perhaps explained in detail why sudden changes had to be made, particularly because the top three customers of the company were responsible for 60 per cent of the business.

Pacing the concluder–producer

Concluder–producers tend to present themselves to the world as steady, reliable, effective, efficient, dependable, organized, systematic, practical and deadline-conscious. They are also often seen as stable in a crisis and present-oriented, which may sometimes cause them to be resistant to change.

Concluder–producers dislike working with people who are constantly changing their mind. They like to know where they stand, what has to be done, when it has to be done, and then get on and do it. Therefore, when dealing with them, it is important to establish a structure associated with the problem at hand and explain the various stages along the pathway to completion. By understanding the steps that have to be followed, the concluder–producer will have a clear picture of the final goal and how it is to be achieved. If you think that the structure may have to be adapted or changed as events unfurl, then it is important to give concluder–producers as much advanced warning as possible, so that they may modify their systems. Concluder–producers are frustrated by last-minute changes, which they see as interfering with work efficiency.

Concluder–producers are practical 'down-to-earth' people who mean what they say. They are usually suspicious of people who 'waffle on' with very little substance to their thoughts. Concluder–producers stick to their word and appreciate others who do the same. Therefore, if you give an undertaking to a concluder–producer, make sure that you can deliver what you commit yourself to. Rapport and respect will come quickly if you can establish a record of 'sticking to your word'.

If you wish to introduce new ideas and concepts to the concluder–producer, you should relate them to what is going on at present and explain in some detail how these changes will improve current work practices. Once shown the practical benefits of any changes, concluder–producers can be readily won over.

Like thruster–organizers, concluder–producers are usually comfortable with conflict and will challenge any issues they disagree with. If you have disagreements, try to look at the situation through the eyes of the concluder–producer. Is what you are proposing practical? Does it upset the way things are currently being done and thereby reduce the effectiveness and efficiency of the concluder–producer's work? If it does, you should indicate that you understand how the concluder–producer must feel with his standard way of working being changed, but then go on and explain the wider view of why you are proposing these changes and how in the long run they will lead to greater competitiveness and efficiency.

If you are a concluder–producer yourself, you will enjoy the company of other concluder–producers and frequently establish a natural rapport. However, you should recognize that your 'converging' approach to problem-solving could cause you to overlook important innovative approaches. You need to be aware of this tendency and compensate periodically by taking on the role of 'Devil's advocate'.

Pacing the creator–innovator

Creator–innovators tend to present themselves to the world as imaginative, intuitive, future-oriented, flexible and independent. They are also sometimes seen as vague, absent-minded, disorganized and critical.

Creator–innovators enjoy working with a high level of ambiguity and will often put off making decisions until the very last minute. Therefore in initial dealings you should appreciate that they want time to explore ideas fully before being forced into action. They prefer working in small groups and will often keep their more exciting ideas to themselves until they have had a chance to ponder them. Therefore in initial discussions they may appear vague, but often it is because they are holding back information they will use as a 'surprise' element later on.

It is particularly important to listen well to creator–innovators and show some enthusiasm for their ideas. Often they will not be forthcoming, however, unless you can show them that you have some knowledge of the area under discussion. Therefore you will need to research the areas under discussion properly, otherwise creator–innovators may dismiss you as being unworthy of their attention. This sometimes causes them to be seen as rude or arrogant.

You need to appreciate that creator–innovators do not work in a structured way and will often give the appearance of being disorganized. Although they recognize the importance of structure, they are often unable to set this up themselves. Therefore they will appreciate someone who will do this for them, will show an interest in their ideas and help them to take things a stage further. Try questioning them in a knowledgeable way about their ideas and ask them how you can help. Offer to help them to develop the details further and watch their eyes 'light up'.

Because creator–innovators are very possessive of their ideas, you need to be sure that you don't take over the situation and use their ideas for your own advancement. Creator–innovators particularly enjoy 'positive stroking' and public recognition, and you should remember to give them a 'pat on the back', particularly in front of senior management.

Because creator–innovators are highly flexible in their approach, they are poor at working to deadlines and to rules and regulations. Often they don't fit in too well to the organizational structure, preferring to move at their own pace and in their own direction. This is often very frustrating to such people as concluder–producers, but because creator–innovators are often the source of multi-million dollar ideas, a fair degree of tolerance is required in your approach. Appreciate that they may be late for work or for a meeting but will often work long hours when considering a new concept.

Like explorer–promoters, creator–innovators are sometimes forgetful. Therefore, if you reach an important agreement with them, make sure you put it in writing and keep a record of it. This can prevent problems later on when the creator–innovator may deny that a particular course of action was agreed.

When opening a conversation with a creator–innovator, concentrate on the 'How' questions first. The 'What' and 'When' they will prefer to leave to you, and if you offer to do this, you will establish a strong bond.

Sometimes creator–innovators will use jargon in their conversations with you, often to put you off a particular line of questioning. Be humble with them, indicating that you don't have the same knowledge as them but would appreciate their talking through their ideas in a simple way. Don't pretend you understand when you don't – creator–innovators are not fooled by people who pretend to have knowledge.

If you are a creator–innovator, you will enjoy working with other creator–innovators, but you need to be aware that differing ideas may lead to competition and thereby nullify the effect of teamwork. If you are managing a group of creator–innovators, you will need all your skills to ensure that they all pull in the same direction.

Pacing the upholder–maintainer

Upholder–maintainers tend to present themselves to the world as quiet, conscientious, traditional, supportive, beliefs-based, reserved and consensus-seeking. They can even be self-effacing and conflict-avoiding, except when their fundamental beliefs and values are threatened. Then they become 'immovable' and may well adopt a 'Defender-of-the-Faith' role.

Like reporter–advisers, upholder–maintainers have a strong value system and tend to evaluate situations by the 'feel' of them. Therefore in establishing a rapport it is important to show you understand their values and beliefs and not dismiss them as inconsequential. Upholder–maintainers cannot do business with people they do not like, unlike, say, assessor–developers or thruster–organizers, who will deal with anyone if there is an advantage in it. Therefore in dealing with an upholder–

maintainer take time to establish a strong personal relationship by sharing your interests and aspirations. It is particularly important to use Operational Pacing (see the next chapter for details) with an upholder–maintainer to make sure you are on the same wavelength. Being quiet and more reserved than others, upholder–maintainers are sometimes difficult to 'read', and you will need to sharpen your sensory acuity and make sure you are both heading in the same direction.

It is easy to dominate the conversation when communicating with upholder–maintainers, and they are usually too polite to tell you to be quiet. Therefore you need to monitor the conversation closely to make sure you are encouraging plenty of communication from the other side. Upholder–maintainers do not like 'wafflers', and talking too much is a sure way to discourage rapport. Use plenty of general enquiries in your conversation, such as 'How do you feel about the situation?' and 'How does that affect you?' Wait for their answers and show you understand their feelings.

Remember that lasting solutions will only arise if you set up 'win–win' situations with the other person. You want a 'win' out of the discussion and so does the other person. If you can arrange this, then any solutions agreed will have the best chance of working. With upholder–maintainers it is easy to set up 'win–lose' situations unless you are aware of the quiet, reserved nature of the upholder–maintainer, who may on occasions underestimate his own worth and his contribution to the organization. Therefore, if you have what you want out of the conversation, check that the upholder–maintainer has gained something also. Ask him to summarize the benefits he sees in the outcome reached and to indicate how it will affect him. If positive benefits are not forthcoming for the upholder–maintainer himself, you may need to spend time explaining and discussing this point in detail.

If you are an upholder–maintainer yourself, you will get on very well with other upholder–maintainers, but you need to be aware of your natural resistance to change and the strength of your personal beliefs. At least one of the upholder–maintainers may therefore need to become more challenging and analytical to ensure that alternative courses of action are not overlooked.

Pacing the assessor–developer

Assessor–developers tend to present themselves to the world as outgoing, analytical, innovative, sociable, logical, pragmatic and expressive. They are also sometimes seen as intuitive, good group workers, 'product-champions' and challenge-seekers.

Assessor–developers have enquiring minds and like to subject any issues or problems to a rigorous analysis before acting. Therefore in any relationship you will need to be thoroughly prepared and to have thought through the issues beforehand, otherwise you may well find youself 'exposed'.

Assessor–developers are also often innovative in the sense that they can give ideas that practical twist that will make them a success. Therefore in any initial dealings it is a good idea to concentrate on the future or at least on the different ways that the issues or problems may be resolved. Use 'exploring' type questions, such as 'What would happen if. . . ?' These are very useful in focusing the assessor–developer on the issues that concern you but in such a way that they can still use their exploring preference. However, with assessor–developers it is important that you continually relate discussion about 'possibilities' to the facts, particularly if you want to create a lasting rapport. Whilst assessor–developers are outgoing and sociable and enjoy working with others, they become annoyed with people who 'waffle on', talking about issues on which they are poorly prepared.

Planning is very important to assessor–developers and they will be impressed if you can present them with an outline plan or a budget showing how you think the situation will develop in the future. They will enjoy discussing the plan with you and will be particularly impressed if you then offer to set up procedures so that agreed plans or actions are implemented. In other words, if you can put on your 'concluder-producer hat', it will be much appreciated.

In summary, assessor–developers are strongly analytical and listen closely to the content of conversations, being quick to point out any errors of fact or interpretation. They rely strongly on their auditory channel to process information and you need to be careful in choosing your words so that they are unambiguous and to the point.

Beginner's guide
When learning the techniques of strategic pacing, it is sometimes difficult to remember what you 'should' and 'should not' do when interacting with people from different sectors of the Team Management Wheel. Therefore Table 2 is designed to help 'beginners' implement some of the fundamental strategies.

Table 2   *Guide to strategic pacing*

Team role	Dos	Don'ts
Explorer–promoter	Explore ideas	Don't talk about details
	Allow them to talk	Don't take issue with their opinions unless they persist
	Give 'positive' strokes	Don't dwell on the past
	Concentrate on the future	
	Be enthusiastic	
	Record important agreements in writing	
	Be flexible	
Assessor–developer	Be prepared	Don't talk about subjects you know little about
	Analyse issues fully	Don't give too many opinions
	Explore possibilities	Don't waste time
	Be factual	
	Speak clearly, logically and precisely	
	Think laterally	
Thruster–organizer	Be businesslike	Don't attack personally but focus on the facts surrounding disagreements
	Be factual	
	Be goal-oriented	
	Give incentives	Don't be ambiguous
	Be punctual	Don't get off the subject
	Makes things happen	
	Summarize regularly	
Concluder–producer	Be structured	Don't change your mind too frequently
	Give notice of proposed changes	Don't 'waffle'
	Be practical	
	Stick to your word	
	Keep to deadlines	
	Focus on results	

Controller–inspector	Use memos to communicate	Don't 'drop in' unexpectedly
	Send written information before meeting	Don't surprise them
		Don't be over-optimistic
	Slow down your pace	Don't rush them
	Take time to understand them	Don't concentrate on the future at the expense of the past
	Talk about details	
	Think before you speak	
	Be practical	
Upholder–maintainer	Develop personal relationships	Don't dominate discussions
	Be clear and precise	Don't ignore their feelings
	Encourage them to talk	
	Be supportive	
Reporter–adviser	Be flexible	Don't put facts before feelings
	Develop personal relationships	Don't move too fast
	Be cooperative	Don't be insincere
	Give personal thanks	
	Establish harmony	
	Allow them to express their concerns	
Creator–innovator	Explore ideas	Don't be too structured
	Be enthusiastic	Don't force them into difficult deadlines
	Ensure you have some knowledge of the area under discussion	Don't be too convergent in your thinking
	Give personal thanks	
	Tolerate their disorganized ways	
	Record important decisions in writing	

4

Establish rapport with operational pacing

Strategic pacing is invaluable for planning general strategies to use in interpersonal encounters. However, because people vary from day to day in their attitudes and states of mind, we need to have flexibility in our pacing to account for the times when the other person is happy, sad, annoyed, frustrated, elated and so on. We can do this by means of the technique of operational pacing.

Operational pacing is a fundamental step in the first stages of hypnotic inductions, and was developed and refined by Milton Erickson – the father of clinical hypnosis and the techniques of Brief Therapy. In their book *Patterns of the Hypnotic Techniques of Milton H. Erickson, M.D.*, Vol 1, Richard Bandler and John Grinder (1975) describe the process as follows:

> [Pacing] is usually achieved in most hypnotic work by having clients focus their eyes on a single spot and listen to the sound of the hypnotist's voice. The hypnotist begins to describe the experiences he knows by observation the client is having; for example, the changes in visual perception (e.g. the tired feeling of the client's eyes that result from his staring at a fixed point). This description . . . establishes a feedback loop between what the client is observedly doing – what the hypnotist sees and hears the client doing – and what the client hears the hynotist saying. This is, in fact, equivalent to meeting the client at his model of the world – going to the client's reality, accepting it, and then utilizing it for the purposes of the hypnotic session. Meeting a client at his model of the world, pacing that model and then leading it into new territory is one of Erickson's consistent strategies which makes his work easier both for himself and for his client. Any attempt to force a client into something, or to get him to deny what he believes, opens the possibility for resistance by giving the client something to resist.

An example of Erickson's pacing is given in the book *Uncommon Therapy*, by Jay Haley (1973). In one of his cases Erickson reports:

> A mother called me up and told me about her ten-year-old son who wet the bed every night. They had done everything they could to stop him. They dragged him in to see me – literally. Father had him in one hand and mother by the other, and the boy was dragging his feet. They laid him face down in my office. I showed the parents out and closed the door. The boy was yelling.
>
> When the boy paused to catch his breath I said, 'That's a goddam hell of a way to do. I don't like it a damn bit.' It surprised him that I would say this. He hesitated while taking that breath, and I told him he might as well go ahead and yell again. He let out a yell and when he paused to take a breath, I let out a yell. He turned to look at me and I said, 'It's my turn,' then I said 'Now its your turn,' so he yelled again. I yelled again and then said it was his turn again. Then I said, 'Now we can go right on taking turns, but that will get awfully tiresome. I'd rather take my turn by sitting down in that chair. There's a vacant one over there.' So I took my turn sitting down in my chair, and he took his turn sitting down in the other chair. That expectation had been established – I had established that we were taking turns by yelling, and I changed the game to taking turns by sitting down.

This is a fine example of 'climbing inside' the boy's model of the world. A rapport is quickly established and Erickson then goes on to a leading stage where his therapeutic techniques are introduced.

Operational pacing comprises making a quick assessment of the situation and then 'putting yourself in the other person's shoes'. This then acts as a starting point from which to establish rapport. An example of poor pacing is one we are often guilty of with our children. If your child falls off her bike and receives a gravel rash, how often do you console her by such statements as 'Come on, darling, it doesn't really hurt'. To process the term 'it doesn't hurt' she must first process 'it does hurt' and then negate it in her mind. However, the statement 'it does hurt' matches her current model and reinforces the hurt, causing her to respond with 'But it does, daddy, it really does!' Thus we would say there is no congruence between your verbalized expression and your daughter's sensory experience.

A far better approach and one which embodies operational pacing might be as follows: 'I bet that *really* hurts. Look at the scratches – they've even started to bleed a little bit. No wonder you're crying.' In this simple statement we have shown that we really understand how the child is feeling – the cut *is* hurting, it *is* bleeding and she *is* crying. These three facts will establish an immediate pace with the child and from here we can move towards the possible solution we want, i.e. a calm child so that we can attend to medication.

A similar case is reported by King, Novik and Citrenbaum (1983) in their book *Irresistible Communication*. In the early hours of the morning a nursing shift supervisor at a large Pittsburgh hospital was walking by the Intensive Care Unit when she heard a loud argument. The intern and nurses reported that a patient was threatening to leave if he wasn't allowed to smoke a cigarette. The patient had earlier spent several hours visiting his wife in the same hospital and had subsequently experienced severe chest pains. He was rushed to the Intensive Care Unit with a presumptive diagnosis of a heart attack. Strict bed rest was prescribed, as was no smoking because of the oxygen equipment. The staff had been trying to calm him for some time, but he continued to insist in a highly agitated manner that he wanted to smoke. After arriving and getting a summary, the nurse marched quickly into the room and immediately began to speak in a loud, fast and somewhat high-pitched, agitated voice. The staff, expecting soft, soothing tones and perhaps a lullaby or two, looked on in amazement. In the tone described and with matching body movements she proceeded to tell him, 'Of course you're upset. You've got severe pain. You're closed in here. Your wife's in the hospital and on top of that they won't let you relax a little by smoking one lousy cigarette. Boy I'd be upset too! It's a wonder you've been able to tolerate it as long as you have.'

Here the nurse made several pacing statements which matched the patient's current experience. He was upset, he had got severe pain, he was closed in in the ICU, his wife was in hospital, and he was not allowed to smoke. All these statements were factual, and by reflecting them back to the patient with the same sense of urgency as the patient had, the nurse quickly established a rapport from which a solution could be developed.

Operational pacing techniques are part of the modern health professional's repertoire but too often in business they are ignored. Often the whole outcome of a discussion will be influenced by the first few minutes' conversation – if an adequate pace is not established here the conversation is likely to 'go off the rails'.

Friends and lovers pace each other naturally. They have empathy, they listen well, they share common interests and they show understanding. They often have similar models of reality. People with different models of reality will inevitably clash unless they make an effort to establish a pace with each other early in the conversation. How often when we meet a stranger at a social gathering do we start talking about the weather. What we are doing is selecting a neutral subject that is readily verifiable – it *is* hot, we *have* had a lot of rain, the ground *is* dry, the summer *has* been awful and so on. This is in fact a pacing technique that we unconsciously use in our initial approaches to test out each person's model of the world. From the weather we will move on to another subject – footbal, theatre, politics, etc. – until we find something of common interest. If we can't find a topic of interest, we will probably terminate the conversation and move on to someone else.

How to pace

Operational pacing should be the first communication technique to use when opening up a conversation. It is easily learned and will ensure that you get on to the right 'wavelength' right from the start.

Whilst there are an infinite variety of ways to pace operationally, a standard technique which I have always found to work is described below.

Fact and feeling loops

Often the content of conversations can be divided into two broad classes – parts which concentrate on facts and parts which concentrate on feelings. When we communicate, we use various combinations of facts and feelings to get our points across, sometimes concentrating on the facts and at other times concentrating on feelings. These fact/feeling combinations can be put together in different ways, resulting in two fundamental combinations called feeling/fact loops and fact/feeling loops. A knowledge of these is very useful for operational pacing.

Feeling/fact loops

When someone is agitated or aggressive, a feeling/fact loop can be applied to calm the person down so that a useful discussion can be held. This is sometimes called *defusive pacing*, as it is invaluable for 'defusing' potentially dangerous conversations where both parties 'lose their cool'. The basic structure is laid out in Figure 3.

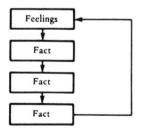

Figure 3   *A 1:3 feeling/fact loop*

In the above hospital example a 1:4 feeling/fact loop was used by the nurse, together with non-verbal pacing (see below). The first comment she makes is a feeling statement about the patient – 'Of course you're upset' – and then she moves into four factual statements:

'You've got severe pain.'
'You're closed in here.'
'Your wife's in hospital.'
'. . . they won't even let you relax a little by smoking one lousy cigarette.'

Finally she recycles back to feelings again with the statement:

'Boy I'd be upset too! It's a wonder you've been able to tolerate it as long as you have.'

The important thing to note in a feeling/fact loop is that the first statement uttered must be a statement of how you imagine the other person must be feeling. If this can be captured accurately, then the feeling/fact loop will work every time. With angry or aggressive people an assessment of their feelings is usually fairly easy, but with other emotions skill in sensory acuity is required.

Following the initial 'feeling pace' four factual statements are presented. The reason for doing this is to establish an acceptance pattern in the other person by quickly presenting statements which he cannot fault. If these are factual, then he must agree with them and a 'yes set' is established in his mind which prepares the way for him to be led by the person doing the pacing to a situation where meaningful dialogue can result. Finally the content is recycled around to feelings again to reinforce the idea that 'at last there is someone here who understands my situation'.

Using operational pacing with aggressive people does not mean that you are necessarily agreeing with what they are saying. All you are saying is that you understand their feelings and the reasons why they are reacting in this manner. It is often useful to remember the '101 per cent rule' in these situations – find the 1 per cent of common ground and endorse it with 100 per cent enthusiasm.

Another example of good operational pacing using a feeling/fact loop concerns Jim Johnson, a project leader in the Corporate Planning Department of a multinational firm. He is doing the '5-year rollouts' and is under a lot of pressure to complete them by the end of the week. This year several of the Divisions have been late with their forecasts and the Accounting Department has again proved to be slow in getting him the cost data he requires. His boss, George Tucker, telephones him and asks him to come in for a chat as he is thinking of changing some of the parameters in the sensitivity analyses. Jim is really annoyed but, being more introverted than others in the office, he manages to control himself and agrees to meet his boss immediately to discuss the possible last-minute changes.

George Tucker is skilled in psychoverbal communication and notices that Jim's cheeks are slightly flushed and that his lips present a slimmer line than normal, indicating that Jim is under pressure and is probably annoyed and frustrated by the impending changes. George decides to use a 1:3 feeling/fact loop, as follows:

> Come in Jim, glad you could come up at a moment's notice. I know you're probably feeling annoyed and frustrated about this year's 'rollouts'. You've been working long hours, the Divisions have been really late this year in getting their forecasts in and the accountants have been typically lax in getting their cost data to you. You must feel really pressured – if it was me, I don't know how I would cope.

Again notice the opening feeling statement: 'I know you're probably feeling annoyed and frustrated about this year's "rollouts" '. Next follow three factual statements –

> You've been working long hours (Fact 1).
> . . . the Divisions have been really late this year in getting their forecasts in (Fact 2).
> . . . the accountants have been typically lax in getting their cost data to you (Fact 3).

Finally the loop is completed by cycling back to a feeling statement, this time as the comment –

> You must feel really pressured – if it was me, I don't know how I would cope.

Fact/feeling loops
When someone is feeling a little depressed, it is useful to try *supportive*

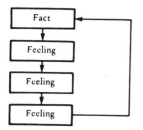

Figure 4 *A 1:3 fact/feeling loop*

pacing using fact/feeling loops. Here we attempt to show that we really understand how they must be feeling. The basic structure is shown in Figure 4.

Shane Herbert is an architect working in a small practice committed to innovative design. His group has been working on design schematics for a new high-rise residential/business block in the middle of the city. Most of the design work has been done by Howard James, the chief draughtsman, who worked long hours to make the deadline for receipt of proposals. The company has just learned that the job has gone to a competitor. Howard is particularly 'down', as this is the third job in a row the firm has missed out on. Shane knows this and calls Howard in to discuss the work programme for the next month. Shane decides to use a supportive pacing approach, as follows –

> Take a seat, Howard . . . You've been working long and hard on the high-rise project. I can understand how you must be feeling now that we've missed out on the job. You must be really disappointed and feel that you've wasted your time. I know I feel that way too. However, the report was well prepared and presented and the designs very innovative. It can't be long before we succeed in a proposal . . .

Shane has used here a 1:3 fact/feeling loop designed to pace in a supportive way. He opens up with the fact 'You've been working long and hard on the high-rise project', and then moves into three feeling statements as follows –

> I can understand how you must be feeling now that we've missed out on the job (Feeling statement 1).
> You must be really disappointed and feel you've wasted your time (Feeling statement 2).
> I know I feel that way too (Feeling statement 3).

This particular use of the feeling statements is known as 'you–you–me feeling', where the first two statements concentrate on the other person ('you' statements) and the third one is linked into your own feelings ('me' statements). This cross-linking feeling pattern is a powerful rapport generator and one that I use frequently when working in a supportive pacing mode.

Finally Shane completes the loop with a factual statement:

> However, the report was well prepared and presented and the designs innovative. It can't be long before we succeed in a proposal . . .

Any combination of feeling/fact statements can be used for pacing. The comments about the weather mentioned earlier are an example of zero feeling pacing and we could use any combination from zero feeling pacing right through to zero fact pacing in order to establish rapport. However, in my experience I have found 1:3 loops to be particularly useful in the cases where a strong rapport is necessary to proceed positively and quickly to the next part of the conversation. Therefore it is worthwhile practising these until they become an automatic part of your communication pattern.

Sensory acuity

To be a successful communicator, and in particular to pace well, it is necessary to have highly developed sensory acuity. When someone talks to us, the content of the conversation is only half of the message. The tone and tempo of the voice, the position of the hands, the facial expressions all give us information communicated direct from the unconscious. By learning to decode these non-verbal messages our communication effectiveness is greatly enhanced.

Recently a great deal has been written about 'body language' and how one can understand the deepest thoughts of persons by watching their hand gestures or how they are sitting in a chair. Whilst many of these techniques can be useful indicators of a person's inner state, they are open to misinterpretation, particularly by inexperienced observers. I have found facial gestures to be far more useful as a guide to a person's inner state, particularly those associated with the external sensors of the body, i.e. eyes, ears, mouth and nose.

Eyes are perhaps the most useful indicators of whether a person is interested in what you are saying. A direct focus in your direction and a 'sparkle' indicate that the person is 'on your wavelength', understanding what you are saying. If they constantly allow their gaze to shift away, say to the upper left, they may well not be listening to you but concentrating on some visual image which has come into their mind, perhaps triggered by what you have said or just by allowing their mind to wander. One of my colleagues has the habit of defocusing his eyes and allowing his pupils to dilate slightly when he has stopped listening to what you are saying. Over the years I have learned to monitor this signal and will 'change my tack' when I observe this happening. Usually a change in voice tempo and volume can be enough to jolt him back to the present or sometimes I may move to another topic, coming back to the present subject when his conscious and unconscious are completely attentive.

Representational systems

Perhaps the most useful message the eyes can give us is associated with what are called representational systems. All our experiences and interpretations of the world are transformed into models through our input channels of sight, sound, touch, smell and taste. In their book

Patterns of the Hypnotic Techniques of Milton H. Erickson, Vol. 2, Grinder, DeLozier and Bandler (1977) explain this by introducing the concept of the 'four-tuple', which encompasses the four major input channels. All experiences can be represented by the vector notation

$$<V, A, K, O>$$

where V = visual channel
A = auditory tonal channel
K = kinesthetic channel (touch and feelings)
O = olfactory channel

The 'four-tuple' is an elegant set of four members which can accurately represent a person's sensory experience at a moment in time. For example, shortly after we moved into our new house one of our sons got his tee-shirt completely covered in mulberry stains, which are almost impossible to remove with modern-day soap powders. As a result, my wife bought some bleaching solution to return the once-white shirt to its former glory. Now it is a long time since I have smelt bleaching solution, and when I walked into the laundry and saw my wife doing the washing, the smell immediately reminded me of washing day when I was little and how I used to help my grandmother wring the clothes through the hand 'mangle'. I could almost hear the sound of her voice, and it made me feel sad that these happy memories were now long gone.

That momentary experience can be readily represented by the four-tuple as a vector comprising four input channels. The combination of these channels defined my experience at that point in time. The four-tuple can be written as

$<V$ = my wife doing the laundry
A = the sound of my grandmother's voice
K = the feeling of sadness that happy experiences with my grandmother were no more
O = the smell of the bleaching solution $>$

These input channels are a mixture of those coming from external sources (V and O) and those generated internally from remembering past events (K and A). It often helps to use a referential index in the four-tuple notation to indicate whether the channel data are externally or internally generated. In this example the visual and olfactory channels are coming from sources external to myself whereas the auditory tonal and the kinesthetic experiences are generated by me internally. Thus, using the expanded system, we could write the four-tuple as –

$$<V_e, A_i, K_i, O_e>$$

which describes a situation where the external inputs are stimuli 'anchored' to internal data. The external data gathered through the visual and olfactory channels cause internal kinesthetic and auditory tonal experiences to be released. The mixed four-tuple then represents my momentary total experience of the situation.

During our life there is a constant interplay between external and internal experiences. External experiences continually modify our internal experiences and we build up our model of the world, which is a sum total of our experiences in it. Each experience we have can be represented by a four-tuple to which we assign some language description – a word, phrase or sentence. This transformation of the four-tuple into an auditory digital form (words) is often unique to each person. 'Washing day' to me may mean something quite different to you, as the experiences represented by those words will be described by different four-tuples. The assigning of words to the four-tuple represents a transformation of the vector into an auditory digital (Ad) format and can be written as follows –

$$<V, A, K, O> \;\;==> \;\; Ad$$

For the washing-day example described, the specific transformation of the internal four-tuple is –

<grandmother washing, sound of grandmother, feeling happy and secure, smell of bleach> ==> washing day

Here I have written the four-tuple as a complete internal representation rather than the combination of internal and external inputs described earlier when I saw my wife doing the laundry. The relationship between an auditory digital transformation and the four-tuple from which it is derived is always one based upon internal data. 'Washing day' to me is an auditory digital transformation I have made in the past, based upon a continual iteration of external and internal experiences. However, at any point in time the transformation will always be one operating on my internal data, for if I say to myself 'What does "washing day" mean to me', I immediately access internal data across the four input channels (V, A, K, O).

Consider now a complete internal four-tuple associated with the auditory digital transformation 'beach'. Think for a moment what the word 'beach' means to you . . .

For me 'beach' can be written as a four-tuple vector as follows –

$<V$ = the sight of waves crashing on the sand
A = the sound of gulls flying overhead
K = the blazing sun burning my arms and legs
O = the smell of salt spray and fresh air $>$

This four-tuple is anchored to the word 'beach' and has been filed away in my memory as a result of past experiences in my childhood. Your four-tuple may be something completely different, such as –

$<V$ = the rain drizzling down on an overcast day
A = the sound of the ice-cream vendor playing his loud 'Green-sleeves' tune
K = a feeling of dampness and cold
O =the smell of rotting seaweed on the shore >

No one word or phrase ever means the same thing to everyone in a group. Language is simply a transformation of our experiences and is associated with a whole range of four-tuples which can vary enormously from person to person.

When people access or formulate an experience, they often do so using a primary representational channel, i.e. they favour, say, the visual channel over the kinesthetic channel. To me the word 'beach' immediately conjures up the sight of white-capped waves crashing on to the shore and rolling upon the dry white sand. In this case my primary representational channel is visual. To you the word might immediately bring into your conscious mind the feeling of sunburn.

As another example, think now of the word 'fire'. What came to your mind first? Was it the sight of flickering flames? Was it the feeling of heat and the sensation of smoke choking your lungs? Was it the sound of crackling flames or the smell of burning? Whatever it was would be your primary representational channel for that experience. Most people use a primary representational channel for each experience, although it may well change frequently as they access different types of experience. However, it does seem that one particular channel is often favoured over the others and a knowledge of this channel can be invaluable in presenting information to a person in a way that seems to them to be persuasive. We shall discuss this in more detail in Chapter 7.

A knowledge of which representational channel a person is using at a particular time can be invaluable for generating rapport. Grinder, DeLozier and Bandler first showed how to do this in *Patterns of the Hypnotic Techniques of Milton H. Erickson*, Vol. 2:

> . . . each of us has developed particular body movements which indicate to the acute observer which representational system we are using. Especially rich in significance are the eye scanning patterns which we have developed. Thus, for the student of hypnosis, predicates in the verbal system and eye scanning patterns in the non-verbal system offer quick and powerful ways of determining which of the potential meaning-making resources – the representational systems – the client is using at a moment in time, and therefore how to respond creatively to the client. Consider, for example, how many times you have asked someone a question and he has paused, said: 'Hummm-mmmmm, let's see' and, accompanying this verbalization, he moves

his eyes up and to the left. Movement of the eyes up and to the left stimulates (in right-handed people) eidetic images located in the (brain's) non-dominant hemisphere. The neurological pathways that come from the left side of both eyes (left visual fields) are represented in the right cerebral hemisphere (non-dominant). The eye scanning movements up and to the right conversely stimulate the left cerebral hemisphere and constructed images – that is, visual representation of things that the person has never seen before (see *Patterns, Vol. 2, p. 182*).

Grinder, DeLozier and Bandler's work has subsequently been developed into what is known as neuro-linguistic programming (NLP) and the eye patterns have been developed further. Table 3 shows the NLP eye patterns which I have found useful in operational pacing.

Table 3 *NLP eye patterns*

Position of eyes	Representational system indicated
up and to the left	eidetic imagery
up and to the right	constructed imagery
defocused in position	either eidetic or constructed imagery
mid-position left or right or down left	auditory digital
down mid-position or right	kinesthetic

These categories are general rules for right-handed people and may vary slightly from person to person. However by putting the eye positions 'into context' it is usually easy to interpret which channel is being favoured at a point in time. See Figures 5 and 6.

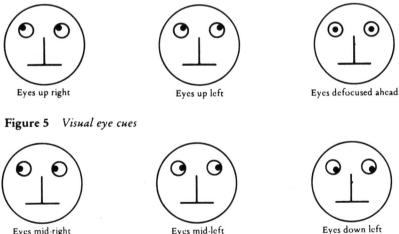

Eyes up right   Eyes up left   Eyes defocused ahead

Figure 5 *Visual eye cues*

Eyes mid-right   Eyes mid-left   Eyes down left

Figure 6 *Auditory eye cues*

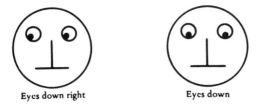

Eyes down right   Eyes down

Figure 7 *Kinesthetic eye cues*

There are two types of visual imagery we use in formulating our experiences – eidetic imagery and constructed imagery. Eidetic images are those we actually see and constructed images are those we 'fantasize'. Imagine for a moment that you are wandering around the office at work, walking down the corridor looking at your colleagues' rooms, noticing the colour of the walls, the layout of the office furniture and the faces of the people sitting at their desks. If you didn't see yourself in the picture but were recalling images virtually 'through a camera lens', then you were probably using eidetic imagery, i.e. remembering a scene as you have seen it before. If you actually saw yourself in the scene, you were using constructed imagery, since it is impossible for you to step outside your body and look at a scene including yourself. Therefore to do this you have 'fantasized' or constructed a scene in your mind.

When most right-handed people construct a scene, their eyes will shift up and to the right or sometimes defocus and point straight ahead. The reason postulated for this phenomenon is that constructed imagery takes place in the dominant or cognitive part of the brain. In most right-handed people the dominant part of the brain is on the left side, and this is associated with the right-hand side of the body. Therefore, when accessing the 'left brain', the eyes very often drift up and to the right. (The opposite is true for left-handed people.)

Eidetic imagery is associated with spatial arrangements that have been visualized previously and filed away in the brain's memory store. This is normally done by the non-dominant part of the brain – the right side in right-handed people – which is particularly good at interpreting patterns and spatial relationships. Therefore, when retrieving eidetic images, the non-dominant part of the brain is preferentially activated and the eyes will drift up and to the left (for right-handed people). Activation of the auditory channel as the primary representational system is associated with the eyes in a horizontal position pointing left or right and sometimes moving back and forth between these two positions. When the eyes are in this position the person is most likely remembering the details of a past conversation, replaying the sounds or content of the conversation like a tape recorder.

Eyes in the down position, often to the right, are associated with the activation of the kinesthetic representational system either in its tactile or its emotional form. If, for example, a person is asked to think of the beach and his eyes move momentarily down towards the right, then he is probably remembering some tactile experience, such as the blazing sun on his body or perhaps the feel of sand between the toes as he walks along the shore. Alternatively, if he is talking about his father and his eyes move to the same position, then it is likely that he is momentarily processing information of the emotional kinesthetic kind. Relating the content of his words to the eye position will give you enough information to understand what is going on.

A knowledge of representational systems and eye positions can be invaluable tools for pacing. Recently I was talking to a colleague who is head of a business school, asking him who might be a suitable person to engage for a lecture series on marketing. The conversation got around to a mutual acquaintance. The head of the school said, 'I saw Paul only yesterday and we had quite a long chat'. As he did this, his eyes moved up and to the left and then quickly moved down and to the right. I interpreted this as an eidetic retrieval of the meeting and then a switch into the kinesthetic channel, which was his main interpretation of the outcome of the meeting. This signalled to me the possibility that something unpleasant might have occurred at the meeting, and since I was after the best possible marketing lecturer for an action-learning programme in industry, I was determined to probe deeper the details of the meeting and whether it had any implications for the selection of a suitable group discussion leader.

I have also noticed in discussions with others that the constructed imagery channel is often highly focused. When people are using this channel to 'draw pictures in their head', their auditory channel becomes neglected and they will often 'switch off' and not hear what you are saying. Therefore an upwards eye movement particularly to the right should, if held for a few seconds, be a signal for you to stop talking and wait for the other person to process their visual images. Too often people will unconsciously talk faster or louder if they experience a situation such as this where they feel the other person is simply 'not paying attention'. A far better approach is simply to stop talking and wait for the other person's gaze to come back to you, or perhaps change your tone or tempo so that you 'jolt' them back to the subject under discussion.

Other facial indicators
The muscle tension under the eyes and in the eye corners is also a useful indicator of inner states, although it is not possible to generalize what different muscle tones may mean. For this reason it is necessary to

calibrate a particular individual by relating these eye indicators and the other indicators mentioned below to known states. You can develop your sensory acuity with your wife, partner or business colleague by calibrating their facial expressions with known inner states. Watch their expression when they are happy, sad, annoyed, frustrated, embarrassed, lying, sexy and so on, and you will soon have a library of non-verbal expressions which will be invaluable tools in your pacing repertoire.

Facial colours are also useful non-verbal indicators of a person's inner state. I have been an earlobe watcher for years. Colour changes in the earlobe are often picked up before they are noticed in the face. People who are embarrassed often show it in their earlobes before the colour wells up in their face. Nostrils too are useful indicators of inner states, both in colour and in the diameter of the orifices. We all know the meaning of flared nostrils!

Another facial indicator I frequently use to determine my pacing approach is the state of the lower lip. My youngest daughter has a wonderful lower lip; it is the first signal that she is unhappy and about to deliver a tirade to one of her brothers or sisters. As adults we still find it difficult to control our lower lip and it can often be calibrated to many different emotional states, ranging from a determined thin lip to an upset fat lip.

Non-verbal pacing
So far we have concentrated on verbal pacing – reflecting back to the other person statements of fact and feelings which match or are congruent with his experience. In a similar way it is possible simultaneously to use non-verbal pacing – sometimes called 'mirroring'. Here we use the non-verbal parts of our body to reflect back to the other person an image of themselves. We virtually become a biofeedback mechanism mirroring their psychic state as shown by their body. Mirroring is a 'higher-order' version of pacing and one that requires considerable practice to perfect. When done well, your body in effect 'speaks' to the other person, showing him that you are 'on the same wavelength'. However, it needs to be transmitted at the unconscious level, otherwise it may well be viewed as mimicry and all your efforts at verbal pacing may be in vain.

There are four components to the mirroring process and we shall look at them in order of effectiveness and ease of use. It is never necessary to use all four simultaneously and I rarely use more than one at a time. The components of the mirroring process are voice tone and tempo, body postures, matching of breathing and rhythm matching.

Voice tone and tempo
Variations in voice tone and tempo are perhaps the easiest ways of

utilizing non-verbal pacing in the business world. People towards the top part of the Team Management Wheel, e.g. explorer–promoters, will often speak with enthusiasm, slightly faster than normal and in a slightly higher pitch. Those towards the bottom of the wheel, e.g. controller–inspectors, will often have a slighly slower rate of speech as they carefully choose their words, and often they have a deeper, sometimes resonant voice. In addition, speech can be loud or soft and the tempo fast or slow.

Voice matching and tempo do not need to be exact; in fact it is better not to be, otherwise you might be accused of mimicry. You should be careful to concentrate only on tone and tempo and not accents, as accent matching is often noticed by the conscious mind, whereas tone and tempo are picked up by the unconscious.

One of my characteristics is that I tend to talk too fast when trying to persuade other people to listen to my ideas or perhaps buy my services. I often get carried away by my enthusiasm. Whilst this probably works to my advantage when talking to people from the top part of the Team Management Wheel, it can be very off-putting to those in the bottom half. Therefore, when dealing with, say, controller–inspectors, I continually have to monitor my voice tempo and say to myself 'slow down', particularly in the early stages of an interaction where I am trying to establish rapport. If I do not have prior knowledge of a person's location on the Team Management Wheel, I will listen very carefully to his tone and tempo during the first interchange and then try to adapt my pace accordingly.

Body postures
Matching body postures is also a way of establishing rapport, but it is also the most obvious and needs to be used with care. In the theatre, matching of body positions is well known by actors, actresses and directors as a way of communicating to the audience a deep rapport between two people. Lovers will lean forwards, perhaps with their heads touching, and *tête-à-tête* conversations are often depicted, with two people leaning across a table, their faces supported by their left or right hand.

When interacting with another person, observe how they are sitting, standing or holding their arms, and try to more or less match their position. If someone is sitting forwards, you should sit forwards; if they slouch low in the chair, do the same; if they lean back, lean back in your chair. However, be careful not to make your movements obvious and do not follow every minute movement of their body. Remember you are trying to match a general impression: 'macro-match' rather than 'micro-match'.

Some body positions are signals of aggression, dominance or competitiveness. For example, if someone is leaning back in the chair, hands clasped behind the head and the right foot resting on the left knee in the 'figure-four' position, the general impression is one of superiority and dominance. In matching this position I would not choose to take the same one but would probably sit well back in my chair in a 'figure-four' position with my arms in front, maybe one akimbo and one resting on my thigh. This would signal that I too had dominant or superior feelings and I would choose initially to signal this to the other person.

However, successful outcomes are never usually reached if both parties maintain their cautious 'superior' attitudes, and I would attempt to lead the other person into a position where there could be a more beneficial exchange of information. I would therefore look towards changing my position as soon as possible, moving to a position where I was leaning forward in attentiveness. This, combined with the other aspects of operational pacing, should lead the other person into a situation where he becomes more at ease with me, and he may well soon follow with a change in his position to one which matches mine. At various points in the conversation, depending on the situation, I would go through a number of body changes, sometimes matching and sometimes leading. My body positions would be a communication with the other person's unconscious mind – a directive for it to follow my pattern.

Breathing
Matching breathing rates is another way of establishing non-verbal pacing. When people are excited, they tend to breath higher in the chest and less deeply. Matching this breathing rate will encourage you to show the same degree of enthusiasm and help you establish rapport. Likewise calm and careful people will often breath at a slower rate, lower in the chest. A match to this type of breathing will help establish rapport with such people. Matching of breathing also has the effect of changing the tempo of your voice. To this extent there is a relationship between the first and third steps of the non-verbal pacing strategy. Breathing more slowly and deeply will help you slow down your words; breathing faster and less deeply will help you speed up and appear more enthusiastic.

Rhythms of movement
Recent studies have suggested that a match of body rhythms can help establish rapport. Sometimes called 'crossover mirroring', movement rhythm consists of matching some movement the other person displays regularly with a different movement of your own at the same frequency. For example, if the other person taps a pencil, you might tap your foot, or if he paces up and down, you might drum your fingers. The matching of body rhythms appears to work by establishing a rapport between the two

unconscious minds. When both the conscious and unconscious minds are in rapport, the conditions are established for a successful outcome.

Rhythm matching is a technique I tend to use only when I am dealing with aggressive or agitated people. I may match their foot-tapping with finger-drumming or their finger-waving with pencil-tapping. I will usually only hold this pace for a short time and then attempt non-verbally to lead them into calmer waters where a meaningful conversation can take place.

It would be very much an overkill to use all four non-verbal pacing techniques simultaneously. Select a technique you are comfortable with and use it as your prime non-verbal pacer. You will find after practice it will become natural – a part of your general skills as a good communicator. You will not have to think about pacing and leading with your body – it will become a part of your unconscious mind which communicates directly with the other person's unconscious mind.

Hone up your pacing skills

In just one month you can become an expert in operational pacing by practising five basic exercises. Do one each day of the working week and repeat the cycle over 4 weeks. At the end of this time your friends and colleagues will be amazed at how much better you seem to listen to and understand their problems.

Exercise 1: representational systems

Spend today looking at the eyes of everyone you talk to. Notice that for much of the time the other person is not looking directly at you but his eyes move 'all over the place'. Try to correlate the content of his conversation to his eye positions. When his eyes are in the 'up' position, say to yourself – 'Now he is visualizing something. I wonder if it is eidetic or constructed'. See if you can work it out by relating the position of the eyes to what he is saying. Remember, as a general rule, upper left is eidetic and upper right is constructed, but many people differ, particularly those who are left-handed.

Particularly notice how the eyes are lowered when someone is talking about an experience which is associated with strong feelings. If the conversation is not about feelings, then ask them how they feel about a particular issue you know is concerning them and note the reaction.

Try to correlate auditory channel recall with horizontal movements of the eye. This is often more difficult to observe than the visual or kinesthetic eye movements. Find someone who is talking on the telephone and watch their eyes when they are listening to the person at the other end. In many cases you will notice their eyes moving backwards and forwards in the horizontal position as they 'lock on' to what is being said.

Exercise 2: voice tone and tempo

Today you are going to concentrate on using your auditory channel to listen to people's voice tone and tempo. If you are strongly visual, you will have to work hard at this exercise, as you will be using a channel that you often neglect.

Find someone at work who is an explorer–promoter and listen to his voice. Does he talk faster than others? Is his voice slighly higher-pitched than others around you? Contrast his tone and tempo with someone you know to be a controller–inspector. Does the controller–inspector talk more slowly and deeply.

Spend as much time as possible today trying to match your tone and tempo to those of the people you talk to. If they are fast talkers, try to speed up your conversation. If they are slow talkers, slow down your pace so that it more or less matches theirs.

Exercise 3: body positions

Today's exercise is to observe and partially match people's body positions. As a pre-requisite, you should read one of the texts on body language (Pease [1984] or Fast [1972]).

Notice the barriers people use when rapport has not been established. Arms or legs may be crossed, indicating that the two people are not yet on the same wavelength. Look for two people who have established a rapport. (The parks are a good place to find such people.) Notice how they lean towards each other in an open body position, perhaps with their arms and legs in an uncrossed position.

Find someone that you don't know very well to talk to. Copy their body position at the macro level, without mimicking every single move they make. If you observe a 'barrier' position, such as folded arms, copy it for a short while and see if you can lead them into a more open position by, say, unfolding your arms and leaning towards them. See if they follow you. If they don't, try again. Your goal should be to attain a matching of body positions in the relaxed, open mode.

Exercise 4: calibration

You have now spent 3 days observing other people and should be ready for the most difficult exercise – calibrating verbal responses with unconscious facial movements and colour.

A good person to work with on this exercise initially is your wife, husband or partner. You can usually tell when they are lying or speaking the truth. What is it about the man who comes home late and says to his wife 'Sorry dear, I was working back at the office on an urgent deal and didn't notice the time'? Instantly the wife knows whether he is telling the truth or not. Why? Because his unconscious is speaking directly to hers, and over the years she has learned to associate those imperceptible eye muscle or lower lip movements with situations she knows to be untrue. Probably she calls it intuition.

What are those unconscious responses that we associate with truth or lies? By using this calibration exercise you will develop skills in matching a person's verbal responses to the 'yes' or 'no' responses signalled through facial and colour changes. You will then be able to observe any incongruence between the verbal response and the unconscious facial responses.

Ask a person a series of questions you know to be correct:

Do you drive a Volkswagen?
Do you have four children?
Are you married?

Pay attention to the facial responses as the person momentarily accesses the information necessary to reply to your question. Watch the eye muscles in the eye corners, the lower lip, the nostrils, the colour of the earlobes or cheeks and so on.

Now weave into your conversation questions you know will be answered negatively:

Do you get on well with Joe?
Did you go to *Les Miserables* last night?
Is John Quale a relation of yours?

Watch the same facial indicators and note any differences between the yes and no answers.

When you have developed a set of calibration rules for a particular person, test them out by asking questions you don't know the answer to:

Did you go to Stanford University?
Have you been to New York?
Does your wife work?

Before the other person responds, decide, using your calibration data, what his answer will be.

By a process of iteration through the three steps you will eventually develop a very accurate calibration of the other person. This information can then be used to check for congruence. If you detect incongruence, it will help you in dealing with the other person by signalling areas where there may be problems between you. Calibration techniques are particularly useful in negotiating, where it is essential to know whether the other parties are being congruent.

People who are skilled in 'fortune-telling' often use a calibration technique to help them in their prognostications. The initial interview will contain a calibration segment whereby the fortune-teller looks to facial responses which will help her in her predictions. As she 'peers into her crystal ball', she may then say:

> I see here someone who is very important to you and whom you rely on a great deal (Fortune-teller sees a 'yes' response). It could be a female . . . (Fortune-teller sees a 'no') or it might be a male . . . (Fortune-teller confirms 'yes'). Yes, it is definitely a male, it might be your husband . . . (Fortune-teller sees a 'no') or it might be your son . . . (Fortune-teller sees a 'no') or it might be your father . . . (Fortune-teller sees a 'yes'). Yes, the mists are clearing, now it is definitely your father . . .

And so the predictions of the future continue and the client will probably go away to tell his friends how amazing Madame Touche is with her predictions.

Exercise 5: fact and feeling loops

On the fifth day you will bring together all the sensory acuity exercises to help you establish rapport through 'fact-feeling loops'. Look for someone at work you know is feeling a bit 'down in the dumps' and try out a 1:3 fact/feeling loop early in the conversation. Observe his response. Did it work?

Now try and use fact/feeling or feeling/fact loops wherever possible today. With some people you will not know how they are feeling and will have to use your sensory acuity to help you out. If you sense the person needs support and understanding, concentrate on the fact/feeling cycle, using 1:2 or 1:3 loops. If the person seems annoyed or irritated, reverse the loop and concentrate on feeling/fact cycles, also using 1:2 or 1:3 loops.

Today or sometime in the near future you should try out your techniques on an aggressive person who has gone 'over the top'. Stick to the 1:3 feeling/fact loop and match tone and tempo. Move them into a leading phase where you gradually slow down your pace, taking the other person with you. You can then move on to the next steps of psychoverbal communication, which are outlined in subsequent chapters.

5

Techniques of enquiry

Problem-centred or solution-centred?

Consider the following dialogue between a doctor and his patient:

Doctor: Hi Bill, come in and sit down. (Doctor notices a limp as Bill walks to a chair.) That looks like a nasty limp. It must be really difficult for you to get around. I bet it's painful too, isn't it?

Bill: Well, yes Doctor, that's what I came to see you about. For the past week I've had this dreadful swelling in my foot. I thought at first I'd been stung by something while I was working in the garden but it hasn't gone away and I must admit I'm a bit worried.

Doctor: When did you first notice it?

Bill: Well on Monday morning my big toe was very sore and by Tuesday it had spread to the whole of my foot.

Doctor: Does it hurt if I press here? (Doctor presses ankle.)

Bill: No, not really, well maybe just a little bit.

Doctor: And how about here? (Doctor presses calf muscle.)

Bill: No that's all right.

Doctor: What about here on the arch of your foot?

Bill: Ouch! Gosh, that's really painful!

Doctor: Well I don't think it's anything to worry too much about. If it had spread up to your leg, I would have been a bit concerned, but it is confined to your foot and I noticed here on your big toe a small puncture – possibly it was caused by a spider bite.

Bill: That's interesting. Here, let me see.

Doctor: What I suggest is that I give you some anti-histamine tablets to take, and if it's not better by Thursday, come back and see me.

To analyse this dialogue in detail it helps to distinguish between those parts of a conversation that are 'problem-centred' and those that are 'solution-centred'. This is a classification often used by my colleague

Charles Margerison (Margerison, 1974, 1987) and is based upon the concept of 'problem-mindedness' and 'solution-mindedness' originally developed by Norman Maier (1963).

The dialogue between the Doctor and his patient Bill illustrates 'problem-centred behaviour' on the part of the Doctor as he is focusing his attention on finding out about Bill's problem. The first thing the Doctor does is to try an initial pacing approach so as to put Bill at ease and to 'get on his wavelength':

> That looks like a nasty limp. It must be really difficult for you to get around. I bet it's painful too, isn't it? (In terms of operational pacing this can be categorized as an open 2:1 fact/feeling loop.)

After establishing a quick rapport with Bill through pacing, the Doctor then moves into an enquiry phase, where he asks four questions to help him decide what the cause of the swelling might be:

> When did you first notice it?
> Does it hurt if I press here?
> And how about here?
> What about here on the arch of your foot?

As a result of the answers Bill gives, the Doctor decides he has enough information to make a diagnosis:

> Well, I don't think it's anything to worry too much about. If it had spread to your leg, I would have been a bit concerned, but it is confined to your foot and I noticed here on your big toe a small puncture – possibly it was caused by a spider bite.

The Doctor's sequential combination of pacing, enquiry and diagnosis illustrates an ideal approach to use when you want to focus on the other person's problems. These three stages are essential parts of what I call the influencing skills model (sometimes known as the psychoverbal communication model) – a seven-stage process for developing excellence in communication. See Figure 8.

After moving through the pacing, enquiry and diagnosis stages, the Doctor then moves into solution-centred behaviour, proposing his solution:

> What I suggest is that I give you some anti-histamine tablets to take, and if it's not better by Thursday, come back and see me.

As a general rule problem-centred behaviour should always come before solution-centred behaviour. One of the major causes for conversations 'going off the rails' is the tendency of people to move into the solution-centred phase before they have understood the problem.

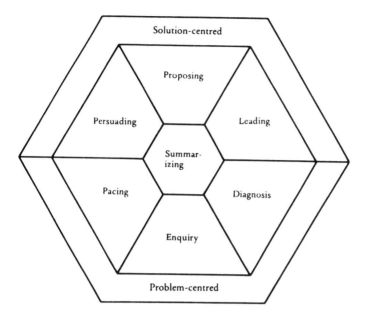

Figure 8 *The influencing skills model*

This can be shown in a rather exaggerated way if we rewrite the Doctor/Bill dialogue as follows:

Doctor: Hi Bill, come in and sit down. (Doctor notices a limp as Bill walks to a chair.) That looks like a nasty limp. It must be really difficult for you to get around. I bet it's painful too, isn't it?

Bill: Well, yes, that's what I came to see you about. For the past week I've had this dreadful swelling in my foot . . .

Doctor: Yes, I can see it's sore. I think we had better get you to a surgeon quickly. We may need to amputate before the swelling gets any worse.

Here the Doctor has paced the patient but has not bothered to enquire or even attempt a diagnosis. He has elected to become totally solution-centred, thereby causing unnecessary worry and expense for Bill.

Many managers I have met are similar to our solution-centred doctor. In their haste to get into action and resolve issues they move into a solution-centred mode too early and usually achieve a less than optimum solution, both on the 'task' side and the 'people' side.

We have looked at the first stage of the influencing skills model in the last chapter, where the techniques of operational pacing were presented. Now we shall examine the second sector in the problem-centred part of the model – that of 'enquiry'. The solution-centred parts are discussed in later chapters.

Problem enquiry

Problem enquiry is a set of procedures for helping the other person fully explore all the possibilities surrounding a confronting problem and to bring out information which might be useful in the resolution of the problem. However, before we look at some of these procedures, it is necessary to delve briefly into the field of linguistics.

When we communicate with others, we do so in what are linguistically called 'surface structures'. These structures are usually incomplete representations of underlying problems, opportunities or difficulties and are full of cues and clues which the experienced communicator can use to help the other person look at a problem afresh.

Surface structures are a transformation of what are known as 'deep structures' (Chomsky, 1957) and are derived from them by processes of distortion, deletion and generalization. As an example, consider the situation where one of your subordinates comes into your office and says, 'I'm having a few problems'. This statement, a surface structure, is derived from a deep structure which linguistically could be represented as, 'I'm having a few problems with Jim Jackson over restrictive manning on the new cranes'.

When someone has problems, they are always about something and/or with someone. The subordinate chose to use a deletion transformation when he made his first statement. A deletion such as this may be deliberate or it may be unconscious. The subordinate may well be 'testing the water' to see whether now is the right time to bring up the matter. If you then use a pacing approach, followed up with problem enquiry, you will be well on the way to a fruitful discussion. The technique of problem-centred enquiry is one which focuses on the cues and clues in the conversation and systematically attempts to extract all relevant issues concerning the matter at hand. Later in this chapter we shall look at a structured technique for doing this.

When there is a deletion transformation, as given in the above example, the procedure to follow is one which will recover the deleted material. Two possible responses might be 'Who are you having a problem with?' or 'What's your problem?'

Both responses are factual enquiries but they differ substantially in scope. The first response is known as a *specific enquiry* or sometimes as a closed-ended question, since it is designed to converge on an answer, i.e. Jim Jackson. Other similar specific enquiries would be those designed to elicit the answer 'yes' or 'no'. The second response is known as *general enquiry* or sometimes as open-ended questioning, since it is designed to produce a diverging answer: for example, a possible reply to the question 'What's your problem?' might be:

> Well I'm having difficulties over the new restrictive manning practices the union has recently introduced for the new cranes. Some of the people are just being bloody-minded about the whole thing.

Facts and feelings

As with operational pacing, it is useful to divide the classes of enquiry into those concerned with facts and those concerned with feelings. Combining these with specific and general enquiry gives rise to a simple four-fold visual representation of four fundamental modes of enquiry (Figure 9).

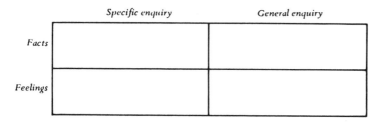

Figure 9 *Four modes of enquiry*

Problem-centred enquiry is the technique of using all four of these modes in a response pattern dependent on the content of the other person's conversation. By carefully listening to the syntactic clues in the surface structures presented and by using sensory acuity, particularly the NLP eye patterns, you can generate fact/feeling loops to recover the fullest possible deep structures. Recovery of the deep structures then forms the basis for a joint or individual diagnosis to be made.

Factual enquiry

Recovery of a person's deep structure is largely dependent on correct application of factual-enquiry techniques. Fortunately Bandler and Grinder in their book *The Structure of Magic*, Vol. 1, have developed a meta-model for doing this, based upon the work of Chomsky (1957, 1965). In my work with managers I have adapted their original model to a format which is better suited to the field of management development. This factual-enquiry model is a hierarchical set of rules designed to trigger appropriate responses from the listener when presented with various surface structures. Many of the rules are intuitively applied by excellent communicators who are often described as 'having a way with people'. However, everyone can learn to be an excellent communicator by applying all the principles of psychoverbal communication, particularly those concerned with problem-centred enquiry.

The factual-enquiry model is a hierarchical surface structure identification set which classifies surface structures into various formats. For each identified format there is an automatic verbal response to be made. We shall now look at the model, shown in Figure 10, in detail.

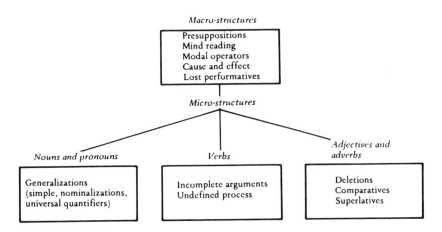

Figure 10 *Factual-enquiry model*

The model conveniently falls into two levels – one dealing with macro-structures and one dealing with a number of micro-structures. Both structures are transformations of more complete deep structures and are derived from them by the processes of generalization, deletion or distortion. Macro-structures are identified first and a decision made as to whether or not to make the appropriate response. Once the response is given or the decision made to defer it, the various micro-structures are identified and the appropriate action taken.

The factual enquiry model – macro-structures

There are five important macro surface structures to look for in any verbal sentence. Identification of any one of these will give you a clue to an underlying deep structure. The five structures are –

Pre-suppositions
Mind-reading
Modal operators
Cause and effect
Lost performatives

Presuppositions

Presuppositions are a linquistic distortion of two or more deep structures which are combined into one surface structure. As an example of a presupposition, consider the situation where a man meets a woman at a party and asks her for a date. In the course of the conversation the man says, 'Would you like dinner before or after we go to bed'. This is a rather blatant example of a presupposition but none the less it is an excellent way of explaining presuppositions, which in this format are sometimes referred to as leading questions.

This statement by the man contains an assumption on his part that 'We are going to bed', and this sentence then becomes the presupposition of the first sentence. The two deep structures from which the surface structure is derived are shown in Figure 11.

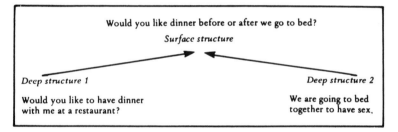

Figure 11 *Presupposition transformation example*

The technique for dealing with presuppositions is to identify the presupposed deep structure and to focus your attention on it. You may choose to ignore the presupposition but at least you will be aware of it. Alternatively, you may wish to challenge the presupposed deep structure by stating it as your surface structure, e.g. 'You are assuming that we are going to bed together, is that right?' Notice that the response here is a specific enquiry directed at the presupposition, which, as a result, is brought out into the open.

There are numerous examples of presuppositions, and Bandler and Grinder (1975) identify some twenty-nine different types in Appendix B of *The Structure of Magic*, Vol. 1. Here I shall mention only four which are a common occurrence.

The example given above is a complex presupposition generated by a *subordinate clause of time*. These presuppositions can be readily identified by the cue words 'before', 'after', 'during', 'as', 'since', 'prior', 'when', 'while'.

Another example is a presupposition created by the use of *complex adjectives*. Recently I was engaged on a 'Management for Safety' action-learning programme for a large chemical company, and during the proposal stage one of the company directors said, 'I think it is a good proposal – it covers about 80 per cent of our needs'. This statement can be rephrased into 'It is an 80 per cent-of-our-needs proposal' and the adjectival phrase '80 per cent-of-our-needs' then becomes a complex adjective presupposition.

The presupposition is contained in the '80 per cent-of-our-needs' adjectival phrase, which implies that 20 per cent of the needs are unsatisfied. The transformation diagram can be represented as in Figure 12. In this case deep structure 2 is a presupposition of the surface structure but has been deleted, since it is implied in the surface structure sentence.

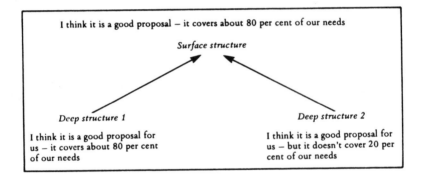

I think it is a good proposal – it covers about 80 per cent of our needs

Surface structure

Deep structure 1
I think it is a good proposal for us – it covers about 80 per cent of our needs

Deep structure 2
I think it is a good proposal for us – but it doesn't cover 20 per cent of our needs

Figure 12 *Complex adjective transformation example*

In accordance with our rules the technique is to identify the presupposition and bring it out into the open with a statement such as: 'But you think there is still 20 per cent we need to concentrate upon?' Notice that the response is a specific enquiry.

Identification of *repetitive cue word* presuppositions can also be useful. Words such as 'another', 'too', 'also', 'either', 'again', or 'back' presuppose past events. For example, if one of your managers came in and said, 'Jones has produced another poor report', the use of the word 'another' implies that there is a presupposition that Jones has produced poor reports before. If you were unaware of this, you might choose to focus on the presupposition by saying, 'Has Jones got a poor record on reports?' (specific enquiry), or if you already knew this and have discussed it in the past, you would ignore the presupposition and move on to another mode of enquiry.

The final class of presupposition to identify is that of the *counterfactual conditional clause*, which occurs with verbs using the subjunctive tense. Consider, for example, the statement: 'If you had taken my advice, you wouldn't be in this situation now'. This statement contains the presupposition that 'You didn't take my advice'. Accordingly, you would focus on this presupposition and bring it out into the open with a specific enquiry, such as 'You don't think that I listened well enough to your advice'.

Mind-reading
Mind-reading macro-structures are a special class of semantically ill formed surface structures which imply that somehow or other a person is able to read the mind of another. In other words, the person concerned believes that he knows what some other person is thinking and feeling about a particular subject without a direct communication from the second person.

In my experience mind-reading surface structures abound in everyday life and are the backbone of gossip and rumours. Some examples of mind-reading statements follow –

I know everybody in the group is waiting for me to make a mistake.
The boss 'has it in for me'.
Everyone could see how I felt.
I'm disappointed that you didn't take into account my feelings on the matter.

The first two sentences imply that the person concerned has definite knowledge about what the group (example 1) and the boss (example 2) are thinking about a particular situation. Unless this has been explicitly stated, it is an assumption on the part of the speaker that he can read the mind or emotions of someone else. The third sentence is an example of reverse mind-reading whereby the speaker assumes that other people can know his feelings even though he has not communicated them to anyone. The last sentence is a combination presupposition/mind reading statement which presupposes that 'you knew my feelings on the matter'. Unless the feelings have been directly communicated, the presupposition becomes a mind-reading statement.

The technique for dealing with mind-reading statements is to challenge them, often using general enquiry responses which ask how the person acquired the information contained in the suspect mind-reading statement, or by the use of simple challenging statements. For the first two examples given above general enquiry responses could be used –

> How do you know that?
> How do you know he has?

For the third example the response might be, 'How did everyone know that?', although in this case you may choose not to respond to the mind-reading statement but simply file it away for later use. In this case it may be better to move on to the micro-structure associated with the undefined process in the verb 'felt', and ask the general feeling enquiry 'How did you feel?'

In the final example the steps are to identify the presupposition, and then the mind-reading statement. Following the model rigorously the following dialogue might result –

> You don't think I took into account your feelings on the matter (specific enquiry to open up the presupposition).
> No, not really.
> But you didn't communicate them to me (challenging the mind-reading statement).
> Well you should have known.
> OK but it is a little difficult if you don't tell me. Anyhow what were your feelings on the matter? (moving now to the micro-structure associated with the nominalization 'feelings').

Modal operators

Modal operators are a special class of deletion transformation in which limitations are put upon the nouns and verbs in the surface structure. They are easy to recognize and fall into the class of *modal operators of necessity* and *modal operators of possibility*.

Model operators of necessity are identified by the cue words 'necessary', 'must', 'have to', and 'should':

> It is always necessary to pay attention to the details.
> One must always do the right thing.
> I have to do it this way.
> People should avoid conflict.

The technique for dealing with modal operators of necessity is to challenge the restriction with a general enquiry phrase, 'What would happen if. . . ?'

> What would happen if you didn't pay attention to the details?
> What would happen if you didn't do the right thing?
> What would happen if you did it a different way?

What would happen if you had to confront conflict?

Modal operators of possibility are identified by the cue words 'impossible' (not possible), 'can't', 'unable' (not able) or 'may not':

It is just impossible to talk to him.
I can't do anything right.
I am unable to manage more than one job at a time.
One may not take advantage of others' weaknesses.

The technique for dealing with modal operators of possibility is to challenge the restriction by means of general enquiry phrases of the type, 'What stops/prevents/blocks/makes impossible. . . ?'

What stops you from talking to him?
What prevents you from doing things right?
What makes it impossible to do more than one job at a time?
What stops you from taking advantage of his weakness?

These general enquiries force the other person to confront the limitation expressed in the surface structure, and together you can both explore the limitation (which in many cases may be acceptable).

Cause and effect

Cause and effect structures are widely used in everyday dialogue, e.g. 'The extra orders over the Christmas period mean we have to work longer hours'. Here the 'effect' is that we are working longer hours and the cause of this is the increased orders over the Christmas period.

However, there are two classes of cause–effect relationships that are semantically ill formed and these result in ill formed macro-structures. Both of these classes – fact/feeling causal modelling and implied causatives – contain the belief by the speaker that a particular set of circumstances is causing some person (usually the speaker) to experience a particular set of feelings.

Fact/feeling causal modelling

Fact/feeling causal modelling is easy to identify, as the statements always comprise a factual statement causing a set of feelings in another person. Some examples are –

Your unplanned way of doing things really annoys me.
Her manner really upsets me.
Their lack of loyalty to the organization irritates me.

In each of these examples there is an action by someone that causes feelings in another person. These structures are said to be semantically ill formed because the person experiencing the feelings ('me' in the above examples) indicates that he has no choice in responding the way he does. This is in fact incorrect, because there are many different choices he could make, thereby controlling his emotions about the matter. In other words, no action by anybody else can force a given response in a particular person once he has learned to control the situation.

There are three recommended responses to fact/feeling causal modelling and the choice taken depends on the situation.

1   You can accept the cause-effect relationship and ask if it is always that way, using a specific enquiry 'Do you always get upset about my lack of planning?'
2   You can accept the cause–effect relationship and ask the person to specify the relationship more fully, using a general enquiry 'How does her manner upset you?'
3   You can challenge the cause–effect relationship, using a reverse surface structure 'Then if they were loyal, you wouldn't be irritated, right?'

Implied causatives

The second class of cause–effect relationships are implied causatives, using cue words such as 'but'. They are treated in the same way as the fact/feeling causal modelling relationships. Examples are –

I would like to do a good job on this proposal but I don't have enough time.
I don't enjoy being stressed but the tight deadlines of project work demand it.

Other cue words which generate similar implied causatives are 'and', 'or', 'as', 'while', 'during', 'since'.

Lost performatives

There is a particular class of surface structure that makes a generalization about the world as if it were true for everybody. In fact it is a limitation imposed by the other person on his own model of reality and results from what is called a performative deletion. As an example, consider the sentence 'It is wrong for people to behave in this way'. This is a generalization being made by the speaker about all people and is in fact a value judgement which the speaker is imposing on others. The surface structure is related to the deep structure as in Figure 13. The deep structure is referred to as the performative by linguists and the surface structure is referred to as a lost performative. The point in analysing the surface structure in this way is to highlight that the surface structure is

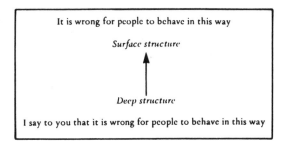

Figure 13 *Lost performative transformation*

only true for the speaker's model and this could very well be a limitation for him.

If you identify lost performatives as being important, the response technique is to challenge the generalization so the other person comes to see that his views are the result of his belief system. General enquiry responses should be used, as indicated below –

Why is it wrong for people to behave in this way?
Is it wrong for everybody or is it wrong just for you?

Micro-structures

Once you have quickly examined the verbal sentences for any of the above macro-structures, you may then move on to examine the micro-structures of the component parts of the sentence – nouns and pronouns, verbs, and adjectives and adverbs. We shall now look at each one of these in turn.

Nouns and pronouns

One of the commonest processes which occurs when people communicate their surface structures is the generalization associated with nouns and pronouns. Being able to recognize these structures and respond appropriately will recover deep structures in a very short time.

Although nouns may be defined in the dictionary, most people have their own localized definition, which is associated with their 'four-tuple' experience of the noun. The word 'dog', for instance, means a loving Great Dane to one person and a yelping terrier to another. Therefore it is important to make sure that all parties in a conversation interpret the nouns and pronouns in the same way. When people are vague in their surface structures, they are often using over-generalized nouns and pronouns which need to be 'dug out' and described more specifically. Some examples of simple generalizations are given below –

Sentence	Generalization
People don't seem to get on with me	People
They don't understand the reasons	They, reasons
Something should be done to rectify the situation	Something, situation

The technique for dealing with simple generalizations is to respond with an enquiry (either general or specific) which is designed to specify the noun or pronoun more completely. 'Who' or 'What' questions are extremely useful here. For the above three examples appropriate responses might be –

Who doesn't get on with you?
What reasons? or Who doesn't?
What should be done? or What situation?

More complex generalizations are associated with what are called nominalizations, which contain both generalizations and distortions. They occur whenever a process verb is distorted into an event:

Nominalization	Process verb
Productivity	Produce
Efficiency	Efficient
Competitiveness	Competitive
Punctuality	Punctual
Confusion	Confuse
Feelings	Feel

'Productivity', for example, is a nominalization of the verb 'produce', but what does productivity mean? Is it machines working more effectively? Is it about encouraging people to be more productive? Nominalizations are particularly vague words or phrases and the use of them should be a cue for you to check that you fully understand what is being said. There is a simple test for recognizing nominalizations – create a visual image of the nominalization and then see if you can touch it. If you can't, then it is likely to be a nominalization.

The technique for dealing with nominalizations is to turn them back into verbs and ask for a more complete description of the process by using general enquiry 'How' questions. For example –

I have strong feelings about this.
(How do you feel about this?)
We must increase our productivity.
(How can we produce more?)
My team is in a state of confusion.

(How are they confused?)
The efficiency here is abysmal.
(How can we be more efficient?)

The last type of generalization occurring with nouns and pronouns is that associated with the universal quantifiers, 'all', 'each', 'every', 'any', 'never', 'nowhere', 'none', 'no one', 'nothing', 'nobody'.

Nobody ever listens to me
I can't rely on anyone
All of them are useless

Whenever these occur in a surface structure there is a generalization present which may be challenged if you think it is a limitation to resolving the problem. The generalizations are challenged as follows, using a specific enquiry in a 'You mean. . . ?' format –

You mean nobody ever listens to you.
You mean there isn't a single person you can rely on.
You mean every single one of them is useless.

Verbs
After checking the nouns and pronouns in the surface structure the verbs are examined for incomplete arguments and undefined processes.

Incomplete arguments
Verbs are particularly susceptible to deletion transformations whereby arguments are deleted from the surface structure. For example, in the surface structure 'I'm scared' the verb 'scare' has an argument deletion. Linguistically the verb 'scare' requires something to do the scaring and someone to be scared. The deep structure from which the surface structure 'I'm scared' is derived will be one that has all the arguments completely specified. A possible deep structure might therefore be 'I'm scared of people'. Therefore to recover this deep structure you would use a general enquiry of the form 'What scares you?' If the reply was as indicated ('I'm scared of people'), then you would immediately notice that the speaker has completed the argument but in doing so has used a simple generalization in the noun 'people'. You would then proceed to recover the deep structure associated with the noun 'people' in the way suggested above in the section on nouns and pronouns.

Other examples of incomplete arguments are –

The union delegate is really upset.
The fitters claim they have been victimized.
I am annoyed.

In the first example the verb 'upset' implies that the union delegate must be upset about something but this 'something' is missing in the surface structure. Therefore it would be recovered with the general enquiry 'What is he upset about?'

In the second example there are two deletions, one associated with the verb 'claim' (to whom are they claiming) and one with the verb 'victimize'. Depending on the situation, you would concentrate on one verb and respond accordingly with, say, 'Who do they consider are victimizing them?'

The last example has a single argument deletion associated with the verb 'annoy' and the appropriate response would be 'Who/what is annoying you?'

Undefined process

Back in my primary school days I was taught that a verb is a 'doing' word. This means that there is some process or action associated with the verb and very often this is not completely specified. Consider, for example, the sentence 'Leave it to me, I can deal with it'. Assuming that the pronoun 'it' is specified to your satisfaction, you would turn your attention to the verb 'deal' and check that you had a complete understanding of the process of 'dealing with it'. If you were unsure of the process, you might well choose to respond with a general enquiry so that the verb is more completely specified.

How (specifically) will you deal with it?

A good technique to use is to try and visualize the action or process associated with the verb. If you can't get a clear picture or have to make too many assumptions, then you should use a general enquiry to recover more information about the process.

Other examples containing undefined processes are –

I'll look into the matter.
I'll report back to you.
The production manager dominates his staff.

Possible responses using general enquiries would be –

How will you look into it? (What will you do?)
How will you let me know? (Can you let me have a written report?)
How does he dominate them? (What sort of things does he do?)

Of particular importance in undefined verbal processes is the verb 'to be' followed by an adverb –

I was late.
I am sure.
I will get there.

In these cases the verb and the adverb define the process and are treated together when making a general enquiry

How late were you?
How are you sure?
How will you get there?

Adjectives and adverbs
Some classes of adjectives and adverbs suffer from linguistic deletions and are generally easy to recognize. For example, the sentence 'This is an ambiguous report' contains an adjective 'ambiguous' which suffers from deletion. The sentence can be rewritten without loss of meaning as 'This is a report which is ambiguous'. From the information given above about verbal arguments and incomplete process specification you will notice that the verbal phrase 'to be ambiguous' suffers on both counts. Working on the deletion, you could respond with the specific enquiry 'To whom is it ambiguous?' or you may prefer to tackle the implied generalization with a general enquiry 'How is it ambiguous?'

There are also a number of adverbs which suffer from deletions, and these can be readily recognized by the ending '-ly'. Examples of such cue words are 'clearly', 'fortunately', 'surprisingly', and 'obviously'.

Obviously we shall have to sack him.
Fortunately the report was late.

All the '-ly' words to which a deletion transformation applies can be paraphrased by the words 'it is', e.g.

It is obvious.
It is fortunate.

Where this occurs, you need to check 'to whom it is obvious', and if you consider the deletion needs to be recovered, you can do so with a specific enquiry 'To whom is it obvious?', or better still with a general enquiry using 'Why is it. . . ?'

Why is it obvious?
Why is it fortunate?

Comparatives and superlatives
The final class of micro-structure that needs to be identified is associated with comparatives and superlatives. Comparatives are those adjectives

with the ending '-er' or adjectives preceded by 'more', as in 'faster', 'better' or 'more useful' –

This candidate is more intelligent.
This project is better.

Superlatives can be identified by adjectives ending in '-est' or preceded by 'most', as in 'best', or 'most interesting' –

This is the best person for the job.
This is the most important project to work on.

With comparatives and superlatives you need to check that both you and the speaker have a full understanding of the 'benchmarks' against which the comparatives and superlatives are being used. If clarification is necessary you may recover the deletion with a specific enquiry, such as –

Who is she more intelligent than?
Better than what other projects?
Best of whom?
Most important of what projects?

Beginner's guide

When trying to master factual enquiry using the surface structure analysis approach, beginners may find the technique overwhelming and wonder how they can ever carry out a full analysis without there being long periods of silence in the conversation. Mastering these techniques is rather like driving a car, though. At first you wonder how you could possibly steer the vehicle at the same time as changing gear, remembering to depress the clutch, switch on the blinker and keep your eye on the road. However, it is not long before your clumsiness disappears, and you may end up driving across town not even remembering how you got to your destination. Your unconscious has taken over and automatically made the correct responses. So too will using the factual enquiry model seem clumsy and counter-productive, but persevere and your responses will soon be automatic and you will intuitively know what to say and when to say it.

In the early stages of using the model I have found it useful to concentrate on only three of the macro-structures, and in the micro-structures on only the nouns and pronouns and the verbs. The eight surface structure types contained in these sections should cover about 90 per cent of the situations encountered in management. Figure 14 sets out such a 'beginner's model' as a surface structure analysis pathway.

When you are in a situation where you decide to use problem enquiry, the first thing to do is to check the sentence as a whole for the presence of

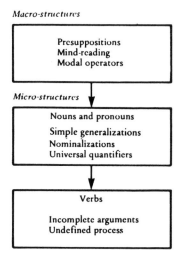

Macro-structures

> Presuppositions
> Mind-reading
> Modal operators

Micro-structures

> Nouns and pronouns
>
> Simple generalizations
> Nominalizations
> Universal quantifiers

> Verbs
>
> Incomplete arguments
> Undefined process

Figure 14 *Surface structure analysis path*

presuppositions, mind-reading statements and modal operators. If any are present, make a decision as to whether you want to recover the appropriate deep structure now or perhaps leave it to later, or even ignore it. When you do decide to challenge a particular macro-structure, use one of the techniques recommended above.

In general, macro-structures should be dealt with first unless they are a part of subordinate clause referring to an earlier part of the sentence containing micro surface structures, in which case it is often better to deal with the micro-structure first. Next check the nouns and pronouns in the sentence for simple generalizations, nominalizations and universal quantifiers, and use the appropriate response to recover the missing material.

Finally check all verbs for missing arguments and incompletely specified processes. Recover the arguments or call for a more complete specification of the verbal process. When all the information implied in the surface structure has been recovered, you may then move on and open up new lines of enquiry.

As an example of the use of the factual enquiry model, consider now a few lines of dialogue between Rod Jackson, warehouse manager of an engineering works, and his immediate superior, Fred Watts. We shall use the surface structure analysis pathway to respond according to the factual enquiry model. Fred Watts is using the model and comments are made in brackets.

Jackson: I've got a bit of a problem (simple generalization of 'problem').

Watts: What's the problem?

Jackson: One of my people was late for work again (presupposition 'again', generalization 'people', undefined process 'to be late').

Watts: Who is it? (puts presupposition to one side to recover generalization of 'people').

Jackson: Rob Green.

Watts: He's been late before? (challenges the presupposition).

Jackson: Yes.

Watts: How late is he usually? (requests more specific information about the verb 'to be late').

Jackson: Well, usually at least 30 minutes (generalization 'at least 30 minutes').

Watts: How often is he later than 30 minutes?

Jackson: Well, every Tuesday he seems to come in exactly 45 minutes late but other times it is 30 minutes (well-formed structure, no other data to recover so can open up new enquiry).

Watts: Have you asked him why he is persistently late?

Softeners

The factual enquiry model is like a surgeon's knife which can cut through to the heart of a situation but it needs to be used with caution, otherwise your enquiry style may seem too direct and you could lose the 'pace' you have established with the other person.

Sometimes it is necessary to consider using 'softening' phrases which try to take the edge off your 'knife' and make your enquiries less directive. There are a number of these phrases which are useful, e.g.

To what extent do you think. . . ?
I wonder whether. . . ?
Do you think it would be useful if. . . ?

Another technique to soften the interrogative approach is to intersperse your factual enquiries with feeling enquiries.

Feeling enquiry

So far we have concentrated on 'the facts', using the techniques of specific and general enquiry, but an equally important aspect to master is feeling enquiry. As with the factual enquiry model the feeling enquiry model also has specific and general enquiry as its major components. See Figure 15.

Specific enquiry to do with feelings is a converging enquiry to check

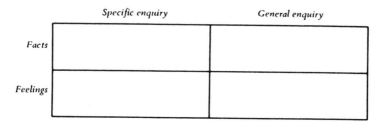

Figure 15 *Four models of enquiry*

with the other person that you have an accurate picture of how he is feeling about a particular matter. The most common enquiry type to use is a direct one, such as –

Are you happy about this?
Are you upset about it?
Are you annoyed by his action?
Did his comments affect you?

General enquiry to do with feelings is a diverging enquiry to recover from the other person how he feels about a matter. The most common type of general enquiry to use here is 'How do you feel about it?'

The interplay between the factual enquiry model and the feelings enquiry model is an important one, which, when done correctly, enables communicators almost to 'weave a magic spell' in the way they are able to recover information about a problem quickly.

Fact/feeling loops

In the last chapter we discussed fact/feeling loops and how to use them for operational pacing. This loop theory is also very important in problem enquiry, although it is not possible to generalize on an optimum loop structure. The important thing to note is that zero feeling loops should always be avoided. Zero feeling loops define an open loop structure which concentrates entirely on factual enquiry. Such a structure may well be used successfully by police interrogators, but it is off-putting to someone you are trying to help. Therefore you should be aware of the time you are spending in the factual enquiry sector of Figure 15 and frequently drop down into the feeling enquiry sector, using either a specific or, preferably, a general enquiry.

When operating in the problem enquiry sector of the influencing skills model, it is particularly important to use sensory acuity, especially the NLP eye patterns. If you see a downwards eye movement in association with a particular phrase, it should be a cue for you to move down into the feeling enquiry sector and respond with a general enquiry such as 'How do you feel about that?'

To conclude this chapter let us see how the factual and feeling enquiry models can interact to 'weave a magic spell'. Let's continue the dialogue between Rod Jackson and Fred Watts and see where it takes us –

> *Jackson*: Yes, of course, but he is a bit evasive about it all (undefined process 'to be evasive', generalization 'about it all').
>
> *Watts*: How is he evasive? (response to undefined verbal process).
>
> *Jackson*: Well he says that he has other commitments outside work and that sometimes he is not able to get here on time (nominalization in 'commitments', modal operator of possibility in 'not able to get here on time').
>
> *Watts*: How is he committed to outside work? (the model operator is a macro-structure depending upon the nominalization and therefore the nominalization takes precedence).
>
> *Jackson*: Well I'm not completely sure – when we discuss the matter things don't always go the way they should. (There are several micro-structures in this sentence which could be dealt with – undefined process 'to be sure', generalizations in 'matter' and 'things', and undefined process in 'go the way they should'. Fred Watts has also noticed a downwards eye movement as Rod Jackson makes this statement – a cue for him to explore the feelings associated with the discussions between Green and Jackson).
>
> *Watts*: Why, what happens? (Watts chooses to ask for more information associated with the undefined verbal process 'go the way they should').
>
> *Jackson*: Well we seem to have difficulty in communicating (nominalization in 'difficulty', undefined process associated with 'to communicate'. Again there is a downwards eye movement).
>
> *Watts*: How do you feel about your discussions with Green? (Watts now decides to leave his factual enquiry mode and drop down into a feeling enquiry mode).
>
> *Jackson*: Well actually I feel pretty upset about them. He has such an aggressive manner and really I have great difficulty in handling the situation (this last comment of Jackson's opens a 'Pandora's Box', as his real problem is his inability to handle conflict situations, as the dialogue would show if we continued it on further).

6

Diagnosis and summarizing

Diagnosis

After sufficient time has been spent in the problem-enquiry sector, recovering and discovering information about the problem under discussion, a move can be made to the diagnosis section. In the 'Doctor' example of the last chapter, the Doctor did this after he paced the client, Bill, and after he asked a number of questions to ascertain the extent of the pain. He responded (p. 59) with his diagnosis –

> Well I don't think it's anything to worry too much about. If it had spread to your leg, I would have been a bit concerned, but it is confined to your foot and I noticed here on your big toe a small puncture – possibly it was caused by a spider bite.

Diagnosing responses are often used in the latter stage of a problem-centred conversation to transmit our interpretation of the problem or at least narrow it down to areas we consider are important. In its simplest form a diagnosis response is a statement indicating the cause or reason for something occurring. Common examples of this type of statement are –

> The reason for that is . . .
> In my view the cause of the problem is . . .

These simple diagnosis statements indicate to the listener where the speaker considers the basis of a problem to be.

As an example of diagnosis, consider the case of Paul Reid, who works in the technical section of a company and is responsible for the production of specialist reports on technical matters. He reports directly to Peter Furzer. During the past 2 months his work has been of poor quality and he has missed deadlines. He has had several discussions with his boss, who calls him in for one more. Part of the dialogue goes as follows –

> *Reid*: I consider my work is as good as everyone else's. The projects I
> have had have been more difficult and I have had less help. I just
> don't seem to be able to meet the deadlines you set.
>
> *Furzer*: Well, Paul, I have been watching you closely over the last few
> months and it seems to me that the problem lies in the area of work
> allocation.

Here Furzer is confident of his facts and moves straight into the diagnosis
sector, using a simple diagnosis to indicate his viewpoint. Of course his
diagnosis may not be accepted by Reid, and in this case Furzer may have
to revert to problem enquiry to find out why Reid rejects work allocation
as a possible cause, or even to pacing if his simple diagnosis upsets Reid.

Personally I tend not to use simple diagnosis a great deal, but prefer to
use a *leading diagnosis*, which is really part way between the diagnosis
and leading sectors on the influencing skills model. Rather than overtly
indicate what I consider the problem to be, I will often lead people in that
direction and let them come up with the diagnosis themselves. As an
example of this, let's look at a different set of responses from Furzer and
Reid –

> *Furzer*: Yes I can understand how you feel – I had a similar problem
> when I was your age.
>
> *Reid*: Did you?
>
> *Furzer*: Well I had great difficulties in sorting out my priorities and
> being able to allocate work to others.
>
> *Reid*: Yes, I suppose that is really the heart of my problem. Tell me,
> what did you do about it?

Here Furzer has skilfully avoided making the direct simple diagnosis and
introduced a leading diagnosis by pivoting the conversation on to a
problem he had when he was younger, working in the same job. Rather
than say outright that the problem is one of work allocation, he has led
Reid in this direction and allowed him to consider whether this potential
diagnosis might apply to him. The use of a leading diagnosis is extremely
valuable when you are dealing with 'prickly' people who might readily
get upset at the thought of your telling them what their problem is. By
allowing them to come up with the diagnosis, you let them 'own' it and
they will therefore more readily accept any solutions which are
ultimately proposed.

Summarizing

In the centre of the influencing skills model is the sector of summarizing.
It is so positioned because summarizing can focus either on problems or
solutions.

Summarizing statements help tie together the fragments of a conversation into a meaningful unit and serve as 'signposts' along the conversation route, so that the speaker and the listener can check that they are 'travelling the same path'.

Some typical opening summarizing statements might be –

Now let me see if I've understood what you are saying . . .
What you've said so far is . . .
Now just recapping on what we've said so far . . .

Summarizing is absolutely necessary in conflict situations where a satisfactory solution to a problem is being sought by both parties. It is also mandatory when discussions are being held with large groups, particularly where issues are complex and speakers are digressing.

As an example of summarizing, consider this dialogue between a Production Manager, Jim Lane, and the manager of a supplying company, Ian Payne –

Lane: The last orders you sent were a week late and that cost us £1000 a day in down-time because we didn't have the raw materials for the machines.

Payne: Did we promise to get them to you by a certain date?

Lane: You certainly did. Your rep promised me faithfully that he would get them to me by the date we specified.

Payne: I guess you feel we've let you down a bit over this.

Lane: Not only over the orders – there are other instances of poor service

Payne: What, specifically?

Lane: Well yesterday we phoned for an engineer to repair the extruder and we're still waiting.

Payne: Well, let me see if I've understood your problems. We've been sending you late orders and this costs you money when you have nothing to put through the machines. This has also been compounded by the failure of our maintenance engineers to give you the service you expect.

Lane: Right on!

Here Payne has used a summarizing response to make sure he has fully understood Lane's problem. Quite possibly his next step might be to move up to the proposing part of the influencing skills model and offer a solution to the problem.

Notice that in the conversation Payne has moved direct from problem enquiry into summarizing. Summarizing is a technique that can be used at any time, with 'detours' being made from any of the outer sectors of the influencing skills model into the middle. However, there are two occasions when use of the summarizing statement is almost mandatory –

1 When you have been operating for some time in the problem-centred sectors and have agreed on a potential diagnosis to the problem, you should leave the bottom half of the model via the summarizing sector. This then gives you a springboard ready to 'jump' into one of the solution-centred sectors. For skilled psychoverbal communication users this is not absolutely necessary, as you will see in the next chapter, where some of the pacing–leading brief therapy techniques of Milton Erickson are mentioned.

2 When the conversation is about to terminate, you should exit the model through the centre and summarize the situation as it stands, highlighting action points if they have been agreed.

Semantically there are similarities between summarizing and pacing but psychologically there is a vast difference. Summarizing is a technique used to draw together the threads of a conversation so that any misunderstandings can be clarified. Therefore it is aimed directly at the conscious mind and forms a basis from which to launch the next stage of communication. Pacing on the other hand is a direct appeal to the unconscious and is designed to establish rapport with the other person. The techniques of pacing (e.g. fact/feeling loops) may appear on the surface to be summarizing statements but underneath they are carefully constructed to establish quick rapport by showing the other person that you have an intimate understanding of his current model of the world.

Problem-centred conversation in action

To finish off our discussions on problem-centred techniques it may be worthwhile to look at a dialogue where some of the four sectors of pacing, enquiry, diagnosis and summarizing are used.

Consider the situation where Sam Weber is a salesman in a retail business. He has been with the company for three years and is a 'rep' for the Northern Region. He reports directly to Ron Eager, the Sales Manager, but also works closely with the Northern Regional Manager in a matrix structure. Sam Weber is passing the door of Ron Eager's office and the following dialogue results –

> *Eager*: Sam, do you have a minute? I need to discuss a couple of things.
> *Weber*: Sure. I've got half an hour before I leave for my appointment. (Eager is skilled in strategic pacing and knows that Weber is an explorer–promoter. He therefore understands that Weber rather likes 'talking off the top of his head' and doesn't mind unscheduled meetings.)

Eager: The main issue is the performance review. As you know, Personnel has introduced this new system and I have to give a written review on all my team.

Weber: Yes I saw the announcement in the staff newspaper. What does it mean?

Eager: Well, each year from now on everyone will have their performance reviewed and a record kept. Before doing your appraisal, I thought I would ask what you thought of the scheme.

Weber (raising voice): I would have thought a review of salesmen is just a waste of time. It is clear to everyone if they are making sales or not. It's just another example of bureaucracy gone rampant! (Eager now recognizes he has a problem in getting acceptance of the appraisal system and this triggers him into the influencing skills model. He starts with a feeling/fact pace.)

Eager (matching voice): I know you and the other salesmen must be a bit annoyed about the system. We're under-staffed at the moment and over-worked, and office systems and procedures interrupt your selling time, thereby reducing commissions. I get annoyed by them also but in this case I think the appraisal system will give you a few benefits (notice the 1:3 feeling/fact loop used to pace aggressiveness).

Weber (calming down and showing interest): What benefits?

Eager: Well it's an opportunity to talk over not only the past but what might happen in the future – where you see your career going, where you would like to be in 5 years' time, how things might be improved and so on. (Eager focuses the conversation towards the future – an important strategic move when conversing with explorer-promoters.)

Weber: Well that sounds pretty good to me. It would give me an opportunity to talk about a few problems I'm having.

Eager: What problems? (Eager recognizes a noun generalization of 'problem' and uses a general enquiry to recover more information.)

Weber: I'm not sure this is the right time to talk about them.

Eager (showing concern): Sam, if you've got a problem you're concerned about, then I've got the time – that's what I'm here for, to help you solve problems anytime, anyplace. How can I help? (Eager notices through his sensory acuity that Weber has a serious problem that has been causing him concern. He therefore paces that concern and indicates that he has a 'receptive ear'.)

Weber: Well it's just that I have this difficulty in getting on with the Northern Regional Manager.

Eager: Why are things difficult? (Eager registers the nominalization 'difficulty' and responds accordingly.)

Weber: Well we just don't seem to get on.

Eager: How don't you get on? (Eager requests more information about the unspecified verb 'to get on'.)

Weber: Well it's his aggressive manner and attitude. He really makes me see red.

Eager: Do you always see red when you interact with him? (Eager elects to make a level 1 response to ill formed causal modelling.)

Weber: Now I do but it wasn't always the case. We used to get on really well – we live in the same street but lately things have been different.

Eager: When did you notice a change? (Eager chooses to focus on an '-ly' adverb and request a more complete specification.)

Weber: Well it all happened a month ago at a party at our place. He accused me of paying too much attention to his wife. We'd had a bit to drink and I'm afraid I pushed him into the swimming pool. Since then he's made life difficult for me. I'm even thinking of changing jobs.

Eager: Look Sam, this is serious. You're one of our top producers and we don't want to lose you over a personal incident like this. Now let me just get this clear. You and Brad Dickson had an altercation at one of your parties which resulted in him falling into the swimming pool. Both of you were probably a little tipsy, right? As a result Dickson has taken every opportunity to make life difficult for you in the region and this is affecting your performance and motivation. (Eager summarizes all that he knows about the problem just to check that he hasn't missed anything.)

Weber: That's about the size of it.

Eager: Sam, how would you feel if I spoke to the General Manager about this. I really need to involve him if we are going to resolve this issue. As you know Dickson and I are at the same level. (Eager realizes that he cannot resolve the problem by himself and makes a proposal to bring in the GM.)

Weber: That's fine by me but I think I should be involved in any discussions – I don't want things being done behind my back.

Eager: Yes, I understand, Sam. I'll talk to the GM this afternoon and let you know straight away what he thinks. (Eager finishes with a final summary statement of his proposed action.)

Exercise

In order to become naturally proficient at psychoverbal communication it is necessary to practise the skills of problem-centred communication until you can do them without thinking. An exercise I found useful when developing these techniques was to set aside one communication session each day where I would consciously apply the problem-centred influencing skills, starting with pacing and then moving deliberately counter-clockwise through to diagnosis. Summarizing was interspersed in various places as necessary. If at any stage I felt I had 'lost pace', I would go back and start the cycle again. I never tried to enter the solution-centred part of the model on this 'once a day' session and perhaps the person I was communicating with thought I was a little weird. I know my wife did on more than one occasion! However, I found the practice to be of immense value and I recommend it as a way of developing expertise quickly.

7

How to lead people towards solutions

In the last three chapters we have looked in detail at the three fundamental components of problem-centred communication – pacing, enquiry and diagnosis. Together with summarizing, these skills will enable you to establish a rapport with the other person and get to the bottom of any problem in a very short time. Once you feel that the problem has been identified and an agreed diagnosis made, then you may consider moving

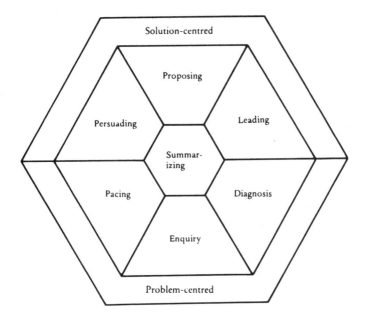

Figure 16 *The influencing skills model*

to the top of the influencing skills model (Figure 16) ready to use the skills of leading, proposing and persuading.

These three skills focus on possible solutions concerning the diagnosed problem and as such are referred to as solution-centred skills. The key entry point to solution-centred communication is through the technique of leading, which is designed to lead the other person into a situation where he can develop his own possible solutions and ultimately make his own choice of the course of action he should take. It is not always an easy technique to learn, as it needs to operate below the level of conscious awareness to be successful.

A good example of leading can be shown in the case where your daughter falls off a bicycle and hurts herself. We originally looked at this example earlier in Chapter 4. A possible pacing response was suggested as follows –

I bet that *really* hurts. Look at the scratches – they've even started to bleed a little bit. No wonder you're crying.

If we then continued our response with the sentence, 'And I bet it will continue to really hurt, maybe for a whole minute or two', we would be using a 'leading sentence'. This sentence is designed to calm the child by suggesting that a solution to her problem is imminent. In using this sentence we are trying to lead the girl towards a solution which will benefit both parties. As soon as she stops crying, action can be taken to dress her wound and there is a 'win–win' situation for everybody. This particular form of leading makes use of the presupposition, which we shall discuss later in the chapter, in the section on surface structures.

Here you will note a direct transition from pacing to leading as enquiry and diagnosis were not necessary at this stage, since the 'problem' was to stop the girl from crying so that the wound could be treated. In general the influencing skills model should be followed in an anti-clockwise direction, starting with pacing, at least in the initial stages of an interaction. The exception is when the problem is immediately obvious and quick action is desirable.

The pacing–leading transition was mastered by Milton Erickson, who used it as the basis for his techniques of 'Brief Therapy'. A wonderful example of this is given in Jay Haley's (1973) book *Uncommon Therapy*. One day, while working in a mental hospital, Erickson was assigned a patient who believed himself to be Jesus Christ and had thought so for a considerable period of time. He paraded about as the Messiah, wore a sheet draped around himself and attempted to impose Christianity on others. Erickson, even though he had never met the patient before, was able to utilize the patient's belief to bring about a major and rapid shift in his life. Erickson approached him in the hospital grounds and said, 'I heard you used to be a carpenter'. Of course he got an affirmative reply, otherwise the patient would be negating his own beliefs. He then said, 'And I hear you like to help people'. Again the patient was required by his belief system to give an affirmative reply. Erickson said, 'Good, here is a hammer. They'll be doing construction out in the west wing. I'd like you to go out and help them'. The patient was soon engrossed in occupational therapy – something he had consistently refused in the past.

This is a clever example of strategic pacing – where Erickson arranged his conversation so that it matched the patient's model of the world. Erickson then used operational pacing, beginning with a fact/feeling loop structure, but because of his skill a rapport was generated in just two factual statements and the loop was terminated with a direct move into the leading sector of the PVC model.

Although few people will ever attain the skill level that Milton Erickson had, everyone can learn enough about leading to make it a powerful part of their communication strategy. The techniques of leading that I have found most successful are those associated with representational systems and surface structures.

Representational systems

In Chapter 4, on Operational Pacing, representational systems and the concept of the 'four-tuple' were discussed. These are very important in leading techniques and I would now like to develop them further, using the Team Management Wheel as a basis for defining a person's primary representational systems. A knowledge of a person's major role on the Team Management Wheel can give you valuable information concerning the way you should lead them towards solutions which will help them with their problems.

When processing information, we form our 'model of reality' by filtering information through our visual, auditory, kinesthetic and olfactory channels. This 'four-tuple' $<V, A, K, O>$ thus becomes a selective filter and causes people to have different interpretations of the same set of data. This four-tuple is then transformed into an auditory digital format and the process can be represented by –

$$<V, A, K, O> \implies \text{Ad}$$

where V = visual
A = auditory
K = kinesthetic
O = olfactory
Ad = auditory digital

Each element of the four-tuple and its transformation into auditory digital format can be focused inwardly or outwardly, and so there are eight possible modes through which the input data can pass. The generalized four-tuple thus becomes –

$$<V, A, K, O>_{i \text{ or } e} \quad => \quad Ad$$

Most people have one element of the four-tuple as their preferred way of processing external information and one element which they favour in recovering and generating internal information. These channels are known as primary representational systems and are usually different for each orientation. For example, a particular person might favour an external visual channel (Ve) and an internal auditory channel (Ai) as his primary representational systems. A knowledge of a person's most favoured channels is very important in leading, as the speaker can phrase his information in a way that appeals to the other person through his primary representational systems.

The Team Management Wheel provides a guide to primary representational systems, as people from different parts of the wheel will favour different channels. The arrangement of these channels are shown in Figure 17.

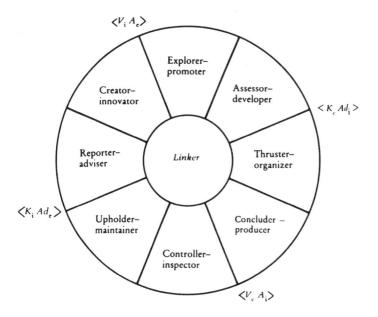

Figure 17 *Primary representational systems for team management roles*

Explorer–promoters and creator–innovators

People with a preference in the explorer–promoter and creator–innovator sectors usually have a strong internal visual channel which dominates their processing of information. Their external auditory (tone and tempo) channel is also well developed and use can be made of these channels when using leading techniques.

Explorer–promoters and creator–innovators are creative in the way they gather and use information, and this causes them to generate a lot of material internally, using their visual channel. When a particular channel is strongly favoured (Vi, for example), the opposite channel (Ve) is frequently 'swamped' or blocked out. Consequently explorer–promoters and creator–innovators are often poor on remembering and interpreting information from external objects. As a result, they are often accused of not paying attention to the details, but for them it is difficult to do so, as their favoured channel is the internal visual. They may make a special effort to utilize their external visual channel but often some stimulus from the environment causes them to lapse into the internal visual channel, blocking out the details of what is going on around them. It is this characteristic that sometimes causes them to be labelled 'absent-minded'.

Because explorer–promoters and creator–innovators are primarily internal visual generators they are often excellent at problem-solving, constructing visual images which help them chart their way through difficult situations. If you watch these people at length, you will notice they use a lot of upward eye movement associated with the use of constructed imagery. Usually the eyes are in a defocused configuration or move to an upper right (left in left-handed people) position as they activate their problem-solving Vi channel.

When leading explorer–promoters and creator–innovators towards solutions to their problems, it is important to communicate with them via their visual channels. If they have activated their Vi channel, their auditory channel will take second place, and it is difficult to get information through to them in auditory format. Although their Ve channel may be attenuated in these circumstances, it is still the best way to 'feed' them ideas. Therefore, when you are describing important information or communicating your views on a particular matter, you need to exchange information in visual format, using visual aids where possible. A simple diagram may be all that's needed to clarify their thinking and 'spark' them off into possible solutions.

Explorer–promoters and creator–innovators often have whiteboards in their office and will use these to communicate with themselves in visual mode. When you go into their offices, you will often note that boards are full of schematics and diagrams which have been used as a cognitive aid for problem-solving. Where whiteboards are not available these people will often 'doodle' their ideas on sheets of paper, as this is a convenient way for them to communicate with themselves.

When discussing problems and potential solutions, it is therefore necessary to focus your attention on the visual channel and look for ways of presenting possible solutions in simple diagrammatic form. Therefore you should arrange meetings with explorer–promoters and creator–innovators in rooms which make it possible to use a whiteboard (or blackboard or 'butcher's' paper). If you then move to put your diagnosis in visual representation on the board, you will then be able to lead the other person towards a possible solution.

The external auditory channel which focuses on tone and tempo is also a strong one for creator–innovators and explorer–promoters and they react well to sound patterns which have 'depth' and 'colour'. They are often stimulated by a faster speaking rate and an enthusiastic tone of voice, and these voice patterns can often be used to lead the other person towards the range of solutions you consider are feasible. A good example of an auditory external channel leading a person into their visual channel was highlighted recently on a television programme about the dancers Margot Fonteyn and Rudolf Nureyev. The choreographer Frederick Ashton was describing how he came to choreograph the ballet *Marguerite and Armand*. He said, 'One day I happened to hear a sonata by Liszt being played and immediately I heard it I could see the whole ballet being danced before me'. Here the external sounds of the Liszt sonata stimulated his internal visual channel into action.

Recently I was in the office of an explorer–promoter trying to sell him some of my services. I was a little tired from a late night and not in my best selling mode. The conversation initially was almost entirely verbal and probably there was little 'colour' in my voice. I was getting nowhere with my proposal when I suddenly (after a cup of coffee) got up, went to his whiteboard and drew in block format the key components of the problem he was concerned about. I became more animated and so did he, as he was able to see how some of the techniques described in this book might help him to solve some of his problems.

A focus towards the auditory digital (Ad) channel is not highly developed in explorer–promoters and creator–innovators and therefore they are not always good listeners. They may try hard to listen but very often some stimulus in the conversation will activate their internal visual channel and their attention to what you are saying is temporarily lost. You can see when this happens by closely observing their eye patterns. An upwards movement or a defocused stare is a sure signal that you have 'lost' them for the moment. You should then stop your conversation and wait for them to return their gaze to normal or make a change in your auditory pattern so that you can 'jolt' them back to the present. A change in tempo, tone or volume will often achieve this.

As a result of a lesser developed auditory digital channel, explorer–promoters and creator–innovators may sometimes forget what has been agreed to or previously said. Therefore, when interacting with them, it is always a good idea to make written minutes of the conversation, which can then be referred to if necessary.

I have noticed an interesting pattern of behaviour that sometimes occurs with strong internal visual people when they are listening to formal presentations. An example of this occurred in a recent meeting where I happened to sit next to an explorer–promoter. During the whole of a 20-minute presentation the explorer–promoter had his eyes focused on a sheet of paper in front of him on which he was drawing the most detailed pattern of circular cylinders. At the end of the 20 minutes he had filled a whole page, which now contained a most intricate pattern that I would have liked to hang in my office as a work of art. On questioning him after the meeting, I discovered that he was in effect fully occupying his external visual channel so that his internal visual channel was 'swamped'.

To do this his unconscious mind was given the task of taking over the external visual channel and engaged itself in structured 'doodling'. The effect was to swamp the internal visual channel so that the mind of the explorer–promoter would not wander and create distracting internal visual images. The resultant effect was to remove competition from the less predominant auditory channel, which was now fully focused on every word that was being uttered by the speaker. Each sentence was taken in with the external auditory digital channel and processed via the internal auditory channel, so that at the end of the presentation he was able critically to analyse what had been said and offer extremely valuable advice.

Reporter–advisers and upholder–maintainers

Reporter–advisers and upholder–maintainers have a strong internal kinesthetic (Ki) channel, and this seems to be the prime way that they filter incoming information. Their 'antennae' are tuned to the external environment and the information coming into them must 'feel' right. They will tend to rely on their emotions a lot when interpreting data, and will often claim that they have an intuitive feel for the situation.

Externally, the channel they favour is the auditory digital one (Ade). As a result, they are usually good listeners and will pay attention to the details of any conversation, often interrupting to make sure that their interpretation of a particular point is correct. As a result, many reporter–advisers and upholder–maintainers are naturally gifted at operating in the problem-centred part of the influencing skills model, and it is for this reason that they are well liked, because they try to understand the facts as well as being interested in a person's feelings and emotions.

Although reporter–advisers and upholder–maintainers listen carefully to the words that are being spoken, they often interpret them through their internal kinesthetic channel (Ki). As a result, they are sometimes over-sensitive to comments that are made and may read into them more than is intended. This will often occur when they interact with people from the opposite side of the Team Management Wheel, such as thruster–organizers.

When leading reporter–advisers and upholder–maintainers towards possible solutions, it is important that you choose your words carefully and make sure that it is not possible for them to misinterpret what you are saying. Therefore it is important frequently to summarize what you are saying, perhaps moving forwards and backwards between the leading and summarizing sectors until you are sure that your point has been made.

However, the most important thing to note about reporter–advisers and upholder–maintainers is that they find it hard to respond to someone they do not like or admire. This is because of their dominant internal kinesthetic channel, which is the strongest filter of incoming information. Therefore, when in a leading mode, it is important to 'lock into' their feelings and move forwards only when you have allowed them fully to explore their feelings about the topic at hand.

As in the section on operational pacing and problem-centred enquiry, fact/feeling loops are important in leading, particularly when dealing with reporter–advisers and upholder–maintainers. For most people an average use of six requests or statements to one of feelings will be sufficient when in a leading mode, but for strongly internal kinesthetic people a much lower ratio is required. Sometimes a 1:1 loop may even be required where you check the other person's feelings about each newly introduced fact.

Controller–inspectors and concluder–producers
Controller–inspectors and concluder–producers have a strong external visual representational system (Ve) backed up by an internal auditory (Ai) (tone and tempo) channel. These are people who are very attuned to what is going on around them and have excellent observational powers, which enable them to notice and record the fine details associated with a particular situation. You will often notice that these people will frequently use eidetic recall, with their eyes moving to the upper left (to the right in left-handed people) as they see a picture from the past. Some

types of artist fit into this category, particularly those who paint or sketch scenes in detail from memory.

External visual people also like to communicate through schematics and diagrams which show the details of something that is in concrete existence, such as a machine or a building. However, because of an emphasis on the external visual channel, I have found that their internal visual channel is usually less developed, and whilst they can use this channel well for eidetic recall, they are often weaker in their ability to use constructed imagery. This sometimes causes difficulties when they try to grapple with new or unusual solutions to their problems.

When leading controller–inspectors and concluder–producers towards solutions, it is important that you initially rely on their external visual channel and use this to lead them into Vi territory, which is usually less familiar to them. Therefore you should make comparisons between the possible solution and some similar situation of which they have past experience. By, in effect, pacing them with their Ve channel, you can then make the transition to Vi and help them see possible solutions. For example, consider these few lines of dialogue between Gordon Mills and Charles Watson –

Watson: We could take a lesson from the past here, I think.

Mills: What do you mean?

Watson: Well we were very successful when we started this business. Rather than develop and promote new journals, we bought out existing journals and then just increased the subscription rate, as we found that the market was not price-sensitive.

Mills: Yes it was a very successful strategy – I guess we should have done more of it.

Watson: That's exactly what I mean. Now that we are moving into selling services perhaps we should consider looking for small consulting businesses and taking them over but retaining the Principal. This would give us an outlet and assured markets and we could probably double prices, using our internationalism as 'added value'.

Mills: Say, that is an interesting idea; let's explore it in more detail.

Notice here that Watson has carefully constructed an image of the past on which to build his proposal. The past situation was one that was highly profitable for the company, and by linking it to the current situation the expectation is created that perhaps this idea could be equally successful.

The internal auditory channel (Ai) is also well developed in controller–inspectors and concluder–producers, and they will frequently recall situations by remembering the tone of discussions which were held. Explorer–promoters and creator–innovators have a reasonably strong auditory channel but this is focused towards the external world. Sounds, particularly enthusiastic tones and fast tempos, will stimulate their internal visual channel, but they do not take these sounds and analyse them internally as controller–inspectors and concluder–producers often do. These people excel at distinguishing subtle differences in tone and tempo and they frequently use this ability to detect changes of mood in the other person.

Because of their auditory abilities controller–inspectors and concluder–producers are quick to detect the insincere salesperson who delivers the high-powered spiel at a fast and furious pace. Therefore in leading these people towards possible solutions it is important to adopt a slower pace and, if possible, a lower melodious tempo as these are features which inspire confidence in the controller–inspector and concluder–producer. An opportunity for me to use this approach came recently when the Personnel Manager of a large multinational company arranged for me to have a 2-hour session with the chief executive. The purpose was to explain some of the concepts of team management and to help him see the reasons for some of the problems he was having. Because I map into the creator–innovator/explorer–promoter part of the Team Management Wheel, I sometimes have a tendency to get carried away with my ideas, and when this happens, my speaking pace quickens substantially. Now as the chief executive was a controller–inspector, I purposely slowed down my pace whenever we moved into a new area of discussion. By calmly letting him visualize some of the problems he was having, I was able to lead him from the 'past' to the 'future', where he was able to use his internal visual channel to see how the model could be of great benefit to him and his team.

People who use the internal auditory channel a great deal often make excellent musical composers as they can virtually hear sounds in their head. Beethoven is undoubtedly a composer who had this ability, as some of his most complex works were done during the period when he had little or no hearing.

The internal auditory channel is also associated with rapid eye movements backwards and forwards in the horizontal position. A public figure in which this is particularly noticeable is James Galway, the flute virtuoso. As he plays his flute, you can sometimes notice his eyes flutter as he hears every sound internally as well as externally. Other performers are more internal kinesthetic people, who almost 'feel' every note that comes out of their instrument. These people will often play with half-closed eyes, indicating that every note is being interpreted with strong feeling.

Thruster–organizers and assessor–developers

Thruster–organizers and assessor–developers have two channels that they prefer to use as their primary representational systems – the external kinesthetic (Ke) and the internal auditory digital (Ad$_i$). The external kinesthetic channel can manifest itself in a variety of ways. Some people enjoy physical contact with others and in some cultures exhibit this by continually touching others during the course of a conversation. Others will enjoy physical contact sports or even get their external kinesthetic pleasures through self-indulgence, such as eating, drinking or sex. Therefore in leading these people it is useful to set up a situation where their external kinesthetic channel is used as a 'lead in' to their auditory digital channel. This can be done by arranging to have discussions over lunch, over a drink or even on the golf course.

A preference for the external kinesthetic channel is usually characteristic of action-oriented people who like using their bodies. They will rarely sit sedately and may sometimes pace up and down a lot. They enjoy getting out of the office and being where the action is.

The internal auditory digital channel is also a prime channel that assessor–developers and thruster–organizers use to process information. Whilst they obviously use their external auditory digital channel to receive information from others, they have a natural tendency to cross over into their internal auditory channel at the earliest opportunity, adding their own internal data to the external data and 'playing it back' to themselves to hear how it sounds. The result of this is that they are not always good listeners, as they are using their internal auditory channel to prepare their response before they have gathered all the external information from the other person. This is a characteristic that can be readily noticed with some thruster–organizers, who often engage in 'parallel conversations'. In listening to conversations between thruster–organizers and others I have noticed on many occasions that the thruster–organizer fails to build upon the information given by the other person in a sequential manner, and it is almost as if both parties are engaging in two entirely different conversations!

Thruster–organizers and assessor–developers are likely to analyse in a logical manner the content of what is being said. They take the other person's words and internally dissect them to recover the literal meaning. In doing this they make use of their internal auditory channel, continually playing the words back to themselves rather like an endless tape loop in an audio recorder. They then quickly make judgements about what is being said, internalize their own words and then respond with their own views.

In leading these people towards possible solutions it is important to concentrate on the facts surrounding the solution rather than rely too much on opinions or feelings. Careful formulation of your sentence structure is required so that ideas are put to them clearly and unequivocally. Fact/feeling loops are important to use with thruster–organizers and assessor–developers, but the fact/feeling ratio should be much higher than is used with strong internal kinesthetic people such as reporter–advisers and upholder–maintainers.

Surface structures

In Chapter 5 we looked at the concept of surface structures and how they were related to more complete linguistic representations known as deep structures. The techniques of problem enquiry were then developed as tools which can be used to help the other person recover these deep structures so that the fullest information about the presenting problem is shared. Skills in leading are also related to surface structures, and various surface structure formats can be used to move conversations in particular directions. Perhaps the easiest format to use is that of simple leading, which consists of the use of a specific solution-centred enquiry and focuses on an area from which a possible resolution to the problem may ultimately come, e.g.

Have you tried using stainless steel?
Could we borrow internationally?

These are direct questions aimed directly at the conscious mind with a view to 'homing-in' quickly on the solution.

Very often, though, skilled communicators will use a more subtle form of leading, which uses certain types of surface structures to seed information into the unconscious mind of the other person. In effect they will communicate directly with the conscious mind but at the same time activate the unconscious mind to recover certain data and pass it to the conscious mind for consideration.

There are many surface structure forms which can be effective in this form of complex leading and the most useful ones for a beginner are discussed below.

Presuppositions

In the earlier example of the child falling off a bicycle, use was made of the presuppositional leading phrase where the following response was suggested –

And I bet it will continue to really hurt, maybe for a whole minute or two.

Presuppositions are linguistic distortions of two or more deep structures which are combined into one surface structure. In this example the 'covert' or 'presupposed' deep structure is 'Your hurt is going to stop in a minute or two'.

Leading presuppositions are constructed in such a way that the overt deep structure is processed by the conscious mind and the covert deep structure by the unconscious mind. If the covert deep structure is recognized by the conscious mind, then the presupposition will fail.

As a way of developing your skills in leading presuppositions I suggest you initially concentrate on leading questions. Examples of this form of presupposition would be the responses –

How can your projects be completed on time?
What can you do to prevent this from happening again?

Both these examples have a covert deep structure – in the first case it is assumed that 'you want to complete your projects on time' and in the second case that 'you want to prevent this from happening again'.

To construct leading presuppositional questions, follow these steps –

1 Identify the covert message you wish to transmit.
2 Form a sentence containing the message.
3 Imbed the sentence in a general enquiry.
4 Decide whether to use a passive transformation.

Considering then the 'projects' examples, the steps would be –

1 Identify that you want the other person to focus on completing his projects on time.
2 Form the sentence 'Complete your projects on time'.
3 Use a general enquiry, 'How can you complete your projects on time?'
4 Transform passively to 'How can your projects be completed on time?'

In this example a decision has been made to use the passive transform-ation as step 4. The reason for doing this is to add one more level of deletion to the surface structure. This is often necessary to ensure that the covert deep structure is not readily accessible to the conscious mind. If it is, there may be a temptation for the other person to challenge the covert structure and a pacing interrupt might occur. As a result, you would then have to return to the pacing sector of the influencing skills model and rework your way through to the leading sector.

Where there is a danger of a pacing interrupt occurring, it is sometimes useful to use a minor presupposition. This involves the use of a 'watering-down phrase' which gives an opportunity for the other person to deny the presupposition in whole or in part if he so wishes. The most common and effective way of doing this is to precede the presupposition with a softener such as 'To what extent. . . ?'. For example –

To what extent can your projects be completed on time?

If the person does not accept the presupposition, then the phrase 'To what extent' gives him the opportunity to reject it by saying, for example, 'It's impossible to complete any on time'.

Hypotheticals
Another useful form of leading is the hypothetical question or statement. These responses start with phrases such as 'Just suppose that. . . ?' or 'If we were to. . . ?' These statements accept temporarily a particular course of action and then the other person is led into considering what the implications might be. Very often this removes a barrier in their thinking and enables them to consider a range of possible options. The process of thinking about these options very often clarifies what action should be taken –

> 'Bill, just suppose that we were to go ahead with expanding our production by 20 per cent – what would we have to do to cope with the output?'

Transderivational phenomena (story telling)
In their book *Patterns of the Hypnotic Techniques of Milton H. Erickson M.D.*, Vol. 1, Bandler and Grinder comment on a technique used by Erickson –

> One of Erickson's favourite devices, employed when the client is in both 'trance' and 'normal' states of awareness, is for him to tell a story. This story, typically, begins with the phrase: 'I had a patient once. . . .'. Erickson then proceeds to describe some actual or created-on-the-spot version of an experience which will be relevant to the person to whom he is presently speaking. The amount of relevance which the story has depends upon how direct Erickson wishes to be in his communication; in general, this will depend upon the depth of the client's trance. Erickson employs the principle that the client will respond best if the relevance of the story is just outside the client's conscious awareness.

Bandler and Grinder call this technique a 'transderivational search'. The client hears a surface structure about another patient and then recovers the associated deep structure. However, this deep structure has no direct relevance to his own experience and so in order to extract relevance his unconscious mind does a transderivational search to find a deep structure that is more relevant. Providing the original surface structure is formulated carefully, the client will replace the person in the story with himself. Schematically the process can be shown as in Figure 18.

Figure 18 *The transderivational process*

The 'story' need not be about 'a person', as is shown in one of Erickson's classic cases about Joe, the florist. Joe was a florist who grew the flowers he sold and was an enthusiastic businessman. He had developed a malignant growth on his face and was in great pain. In one of his sessions with Joe, Erickson responded as follows (Haley, 1973) –

> . . . I wish that you would **listen to me comfortably** as I talk about a tomato plant. That is an odd thing to talk about. It makes one **curious. Why talk about a tomato plant?** One puts a tomato seed in the ground. One can **feel hope** that it will grow into a tomato plant that **will bring satisfaction** by the fruit it has. The seed soaks up water, **not very much difficulty** in doing that because of the rains that bring **peace and comfort** and the joy of growing to flowers and tomatoes. That little seed, Joe, slowly swells and sends out a little rootlet with a cilia on it . . . Those hairs are on the leaves too, like the cilia on the roots; they must make the tomato plant **feel very good, very comfortable** . . .

Here Erickson has chosen to set up transderivational phenomena based on a tomato plant – something that would be of great interest to a man who had loved plants and flowers all his life. Erickson actually forces a transderivational search to occur at a number of stages in the conversation by using such phrases as '. . . must make the tomato plant feel very good, very comfortable . . .'. This is an example of selectional restriction violation, as it is not possible for a tomato plant to act like a human and 'feel good'. When our conscious mind receives a phrase like this, it is considered 'odd', but because of the flow of conversation we do not stop to try and work out what is wrong. Rather our unconscious takes over and through a transderivational search attempts to extract relevance out of the situation. Given the circumstances of Joe, a convenient derived deep structure is one which relates to Joe feeling comfortable.

The case of 'Joe' also highlights a more advanced technique of leading which is very effective if done well. It is the technique of covert commands combined with analogue marking. The words printed in bold in the 'Joe case' are actual commands given by Erickson in a way that avoids rejection by Joe. As such, these are referred to as covert commands and are designed to appeal directly to the unconscious. If these commands are also analogue marked, they will be even more effective.

Analogue marking is the technique of marking out certain words either by differentiating them auditorially or by marking them with some gesture or even touch. A slight change in tone, almost imperceptible, or a hand or body gesture can be very effective in singling out certain words or phrases for unconscious attention. Erickson would often do this by moving his head to the right or left if he wanted to mark something for special consideration. As well as the visual marking, there is also an auditory effect caused by a slight difference in tone as the sound comes from different spatial locations.

An opportunity for me to use transderivational phenomena in the business world came recently when I was counselling a client about modern ways of managing people. Now I knew from discussions with various people in the organization that the client, Fred, was not considered an ideal manager. One of his problems was that he was never available to his team when important issues needed to be discussed. He was poor at delegating and as a result worked long hours. However, there was no doubt in his mind that he was 'the perfect manager'. During the conversation I was able to tell him about a manager I knew. I proceeded as follows –

> I had a manager once who was the leader of a team of five people. He did his job thoroughly and diligently, working long hours every week. However, he was so busy doing the work himself that he forgot he had a team to help him. One feature we all found particularly annoying was his non-availability when we needed him. I remember one day I had a major decision to make on a computer project and I was uncertain which out of three options was the way to proceed. I tried to see my boss but he wasn't in his office; I left a written message for him to come and see me but he didn't; when I finally 'bearded him in his den', he told me he was urgently working on an important deal and could I see him next week. By then it was too late and I made the decision without the benefit of his valuable experience. As a result of his behaviour, which all team members regularly experienced, we used to call him 'Nessy' after the Loch Ness Monster. We knew he was there but we never saw him!

In this response I opened up with the Erickson phrase 'I had a manager once . . .' and then went on to talk about a real problem I had experienced earlier in my career. In talking about my previous boss I brought in some of the problems I knew he was facing, but he didn't know that I knew what his problems were. He showed real interest in my boss and it was obvious that he had made the transderivational search and created a deep structure that substituted himself for my boss. I was able to continue on with the story, telling him how demotivated we all were and how within 2 years of coming together as a team four out of the five people had left the organization.

Another technique to use in transderivational story-telling is that of embedded quotes. In the above story, for example, I could have chosen to continue on with the dialogue as follows –

... well this sort of thing continued on for about 6 months during which time it became even more difficult to see my boss. As it turned out he had six or seven projects on the go and spent his time running from one to the next. Finally he cracked and had a minor heart attack which put him off work for 6 weeks. I remember going to visit him in hospital and hearing him say, 'Look, Dick, don't ever let this happen to you. *Use your team and always delegate*' ...

This extension to the story used quoted material which the listener understands at the conscious level to be directed at the person in the story. However, there is also an interesting side-effect where there is a similarity between the listener and the person in the story. The unconscious mind interprets the quoted material as a direct command and at a later stage causes the conscious mind to act upon it. If the quoted material can be successfully 'analogue-marked', then the effect will be even stronger.

Transderivational phenomena are now an important part of my consulting repertoire, as they allow me to lead people towards a solution without telling them what to do. In the end a solution that is generated by the other person and therefore 'owned' by them is the only one which has a lasting effect.

8

How to propose
convincing solutions

As we move further around the influencing skills model we come to the sectors of Proposing and Persuading. In the leading sector ideas and possible solutions are 'seeded' into the mind of the other person but in the proposing and persuading sectors they are more forcefully presented.

Proposing

In terms of the influencing skills model a 'proposal' is a statement which directly offers a particular solution to the listener. Whereas proposals are implied in the leading sector, they are presented indirectly and in such a way that appeals more to the unconscious than the conscious. In the proposing sector a clear suggestion is made to the conscious mind indicating a possible course of action.

Direct proposals are a way of telling the other person what they should do about a particular situation. There are two basic forms – one that is open-ended in the response that is desired and one that is formulated in yes/no terms and is therefore more closed-ended. Common forms of the open-ended or *general proposal* are –

I think that (perhaps) you should . . .
I would suggest that . . .
It might be a good idea if you . . .
You might like to . . .
It seems to me that you should . . .
How about. . . ?

General proposals are really 'watered-down' commands or commands prefixed by a softener phrase. I don't believe that commands by themselves should be part of a manager's repertoire, as they create an ownership barrier between the two conversing parties. If I tell someone directly what to do, then it is my decision and the other person has no 'ownership' in the solution. However, if I work my way through the influencing skills model, ending up with nothing stronger than a direct proposal, then there is a greater chance that ownership of the solution is shared.

One major difference between proposals and commands is the reaction they engender in the listener. Proposals are phrased in such a way that the other person is expected to respond with his views about the proposal. Commands, on the other hand, are purely 'transmission' devices and there is no expectation on the part of the transmitter that a response is awaited from the listener.

Direct proposals that are formulated in yes/no terms are linguistically known as *specific proposals* because they are formulated in specific enquiry format. One of the most popular ways of presenting these is through the use of the modal operator of possibility, put in question format –

Can you have this report written by Friday?
Are you able to talk at the meeting on the project?
Is it possible for you to work back until the job is finished?

These structures are similar to those discussed under simple leading and there is undoubtedly a 'grey area' between leading and proposing in certain cases. The difference, however, is often in the tone of voice and the emphasis that is used when operating in proposal mode. It is impossible to demonstrate this via the written word and I suggest you say the above phrases to yourself using various tonal qualities and inflexions. As you do so, you should be able to identify ways of saying the sentences that definitely lean towards leading and ways that are more authoritive and lean towards proposing.

Another type of proposal that I have found particularly effective is one which fits into the category of *indirect proposals*. A good example of this can be shown in the following case –

Suppose you have reporting to you a person who has been turning up for work late on a regular basis. Initially he was only 5 or 10 minutes late one day a week. Now he is late usually three times a week, often up to 20 minutes and occasionally half an hour. You have spoken to him briefly about the matter on two occasions in the last month and decide to discuss the situation formally with him. During the conversation he indicates that one of the reasons for being late is the traffic that builds up on the western freeway. Subsequently you make this response – 'Why can't you leave home half an hour earlier so that you miss the traffic?'

This last sentence is an example of an indirect proposal. It is actually a combination of a direct proposal and a problem enquiry. The proposal is 'Can't you leave home half-an-hour earlier so that you miss the traffic'? (negated modal operator of possibility), but this is then prefixed with 'Why' and the proposal is turned into a problem enquiry.

These indirect proposals are a 'sleight of hand' verbal technique to change the direction of a conversation. In effect you offer a solution through using a direct proposal but in the same breath cause the conversation to focus on any problems associated with this proposal. This technique can sometimes be very successful when you are operating in the problem-centred part of the influencing skills model. You may see an immediate possible solution and want to test it out quickly. An indirect proposal is a good way of doing this because it jumps you momentarily into the solution-centred part of the model, but then you cause the conversation to come back down into the problem-centred part.

The rules for forming indirect proposals are –

1 Form a direct proposal, using the model operator of possibility.
2 Turn the direct proposal into a problem enquiry by prefixing it with 'Why'.

Persuading

The final sector of the Psychoverbal Communication Model is persuading. In general the techniques of persuading should only be used after sufficient time has been spent in the other sectors of the model. The best use of the model is one which moves counter-clockwise through the sectors, starting with pacing. Thus you should only think about using the persuading techniques when the problem has been fully explored and the other person given every opportunity to develop his own solutions. The techniques of persuading then become 'the cream on the cake' and are designed to remove any 'seeds of doubt' as to whether the right decision has been made.

There are many persuasion techniques which can be used in conversation but I have found four significant ones which have helped me a lot in my dealings with people. We shall look at these four in the remainder of the chapter.

Sensory saturation
In Chapter 5 and 7, on Enquiry and Leading respectively, the concepts of primary representational systems and input channels were discussed. Use of these concepts can also be made in developing persuasion patterns in the mind of the other person.

Explorer–promoters and creator–innovators are primarily internal visual people who find it easy to construct images or pictures of events and situations which have not yet occurred. Therefore, when trying to 'persuade' them, it is important initially to phrase your words so that they can visualize what you are saying. To do this it is often useful to have a short list of words which can help you draw pictures in the mind of the other person. These words can then be used in sentences such as –

Can't you *see* how great it will be?
Can't you *picture* the scene in 2 months from now?

Possible words to use for internal visual people are –

clear	illustrate	see	picture
depict	imagine	seem	view
flash	look	show	watch

Reporter–advisers and upholder–maintainers are primarily internal kinesthetic people who tend naturally to evaluate situations in terms of their feelings. Therefore feeling type words should be used when trying to 'persuade' them.

Can't you *feel* the difference?
This is the only *fair* thing to do, isn't it?

The external auditory digital channel is also fairly strong in these people and there are several words associated with this channel that can also be useful. A combined list of possible feeling words and external auditory digital words to use with reporter–advisers and upholder–maintainers is given below –

affect	hassle	impress	sense
belief	help	intuition	stress
comfortable	hunch	irritate	stir
emotion	hurt	listen	support
	hear	principle	value

Controller–inspectors and concluder–producers are primarily external visual people with a strong command of eidetic imagery. They are often cautious people who need to be assured that future courses of action are firmly rooted in past success. Therefore external visual type words linked to the 'past' are very useful in developing persuasive patterns. They are also strong in the internal auditory area and appeals can also be made through that channel:

Now let's *consider* the main differences between what we've done in

the *past* and what we are proposing now.
How does that *sound/appeal* to you?

Possible external visual and internal auditory words to use are –

appeal	detail	pragmatic	solid
accent	in-depth	precise	sound
compare	past	reliable	tune in
consider	practical	ring (a bell)	well informed
chord			

Thruster–organizers and assessor–developers have a strong internal auditory digital channel backed up by an external kinesthetic channel. Surface structures which 'play' on these channels can therefore be very persuasive:

When you *examine* the facts, it's *logical* that we should get into *action* as soon as possible.
If we proceed in this way, it will give us a *firm grasp* of the situation.

There are many words which can lock into the appropriate preferred channel. Some of the more useful ones are –

action	concrete	hold	say
analyse	facts	hot	sharp
clarify	firm	logical	talk
comment on	handle	pay attention to	touch
cold	give an account of	report	grasp
efficient			

Communication through the primary input channels is often enough to achieve a satisfactory level of 'persuasion' but there may be times when you have to go further and use sensory saturation. Sensory saturation consists of using a set of persuasive patterns which start off with the primary input channels and then quickly overlap from one channel to another. Consider, for example, that you have been talking with an explorer–promoter and have more or less agreed on a feasible solution to a particular problem. However, you sense that the explorer–promoter needs that final bit of convincing. A useful way of doing this is through sensory saturation as follows –

Well it looks as though the answer is replacement of the machines. Just picture for a moment the workshop with those new machines fitted. Can't you see the improved efficiency of the operators. The new machines have a reliability of nearly 100 per cent and are 20 per cent cheaper than the others. They are almost identical to the ones we have;

the only difference is in the display panel configuration. I feel deep down that we are doing the right thing, don't you?

Notice here that we have led into the Vi channel of the explorer-promoter and helped him construct an image of the new machines in the workshop. Then we have presented to him surface structures which help him access simultaneously those channels which may be less familiar to him. In the above example we have moved from the Vi channel through briefly into the Ad channel and then round to the visual channel again as we compare the past with the future. Finally we overlap into the internal kinesthetic channel with the 'feeling' statement at the end.

Sensory saturation is often used in top class television advertising campaigns. One of the most effective ones I have seen deals with the promotion of an Australian beer 'Fourex'. The pleasure gained from drinking a glass of beer is very kinesthetic – the feel of the beer as it 'hits' your stomach and the feeling of warmth and relaxation which slowly creeps over your body as the alcohol is absorbed. This kinesthetic appeal is paced with the words of the song –

I can feel a fourex coming on, got the taste for it, just can't wait for it, I can feel a fourex coming on.

Visually the commercial depicts a hot, dry day and men doing hard physical work, such as rounding up sheep. The scenes almost create a dry feeling in your mouth. Finally the sound track relies on a 'catchy little tune' that is easy to recall. Whenever I see this commercial, I can feel sensory saturation occurring and I almost want to get up and get a can of beer from the refrigerator.

Visual metaphors
In Chapter 7 on Leading we looked at transderivational phenomena, where a story was constructed to help the other person access internal resources which might help him develop a solution to his problem. Transderivational search stories are a special class of metaphors where a situation that has some similarity to the presenting problem is described. Usually, however, the conscious mind is not directly aware of the connection and the unconscious mind is left to extract the learning points and pass them to the conscious later.

Another class of metaphor which is particularly valuable for 'persuading' is the visual metaphor. They are particularly useful in business for two reasons – they are succinct, and are most effective when used with assessor–developers, thruster–organizers, concluder–producers and controller–inspectors, which comprise 80 per cent of managers in business (see Chapter 2). These people, you will recall, do not have the internal visual channel as a primary representational system, and therefore the visual metaphor forces them to use this channel, thereby allowing them to look at a situation in a new way.

To be effective, visual metaphors should be original and not simply regurgitations of hackneyed phrases. Barry Smith, former Director of Human Resources of a large industrial company, is one person I know who is a master of the visual metaphor. Recently my colleague Charles Margerison and I were working with Barry in launching a major new initiative in action-learning management development. There were many problems in the early stages, as there were several levels of management to convince and there were many obstacles to overcome. I recorded several of the metaphors he used on a number of occasions as a way of persuading various people that we must push forward to our goal. His metaphors were highly successful.

> This project has a lot in common with the Second World War. We've crossed the channel twice and been pushed back to Dover but now we've made a 'beachhead' in Normandy. If we push on, we'll win the war.
>
> Sometimes I feel like the manager of a railroad – we've put down the tracks, purchased rolling stock, built the maintenance sheds, installed the most up-to-date set of signals but as yet we have no paying passengers. Let's open the ticket office and get our campaign going.
>
> . . . we're in the South American jungles not the American plains. We're hunters hacking our way through dense jungle vines but we'll get there because we have sharp machetes.

The time to use visual metaphors is when the going is tough or the situation is so complex that not much progress is being made. A carefully worded metaphor in these situations can often be like a surgeon's knife cutting through butter.

Skilled politicians often use visual metaphors to simplify complex issues. In Australia, Sir John Bjelke-Petersen, the former Premier of the State of Queensland and also a pilot, is one person who did this with great effect. Recently at a political gathering he announced his intention to seek the Prime Ministership and proceeded as follows –

> . . . I liken it to an aeroplane flying upside down with the wheels in the air, with all the luggage falling over the passengers underneath – that's what Australia's like at the moment. We're in a pretty precarious position and a crash is not too far off the way we're going. As a pilot I'd like to get in there and roll it over – get it going on a straight course again.

The Apple Corporation, according to its Chief Executive, John Sculley, is one organization that makes extensive use of metaphors. In his recent book (Sculley, 1987) he talks about the exciting world of computer development and gives a penetrating insight into the *third wave* business world which is driven by the need for innovation. In talking about visions and directions, he says:

> Corporate cultures make great use of stories, generally war stories, repeated *ad nauseam*. At Apple, what's more exciting than myth is metaphor. Metaphor, which literally means movement, focuses on relationships of ideas, images, symbols. Metaphors create tension, collision of ideas, fusion. Metaphor 'gives you two ideas for one,' as Dr Johnson said. . . . The reason we talk in metaphors at Apple is because everything we're doing hasn't been done before.

Inverting the factual enquiry model

In Chapter 5 on Enquiry the factual enquiry model was presented as a structured way of recovering generalized, deleted or distorted material from the other person. These generalizations, deletions and distortions were classified into a number of readily identifiable structures such as cause and effect, mind-reading, nominalizations and so on. The purpose of problem enquiry then was to recognize these structures and respond automatically so that the underlying deep structure was verbalized.

When operating in the persuading mode, it is sometimes useful to invert the factual enquiry model and purposely use some of these deleted, generalized or distorted structures. In effect we want to present the other person with a carefully formed surface structure and then let him extract from it deep structures which have special meaning to him.

Perhaps the most effective structure to use in this regard is that of the ill formed cause and effect relationship, as shown in these examples –

> We were standing there watching a demonstration of the new desktop publishing system and could immediately see how it would cut costs in our business, couldn't we?
> As you read through the manuscript, you will realize that the techniques described will help you enormously in day-to-day management.
> When you come along to the course, you will feel you have done the right thing.
> Just seeing the product will make you want to buy.

These sentences all have a similar construction in that the first part describes an event which is linked to the second part of the sentence in such a way that some cause–effect relationship is implied. This relationship can be weak, as in the case of the first sentence, where the conjunction **and** was used or stronger as in the last sentence where the verb **make** was used. Semantically, of course, there is no cause–effect relationship occurring, but the listener will very often create one in his own deep structure.

The rules for constructing cause–effect surface structures are as follows –

1   Identify the effect you want to allude to, e.g. 'It will help you enormously in day-to-day management'.
2   Select some behaviour that the other person is currently doing or will do in the immediate future.
3   Make up a surface structure which has the form

Step 2 Causes Step 1

The causal connection can be weak if only a weak persuasion pattern is required. Conjunctions such as 'and', 'or', and 'but' will achieve this effect. Stronger connections can be made with temporal conjunctions such as 'when', 'after', 'during', 'while', 'as', and 'since' and very strong connections by using the verbs 'make', 'cause', 'force', or 'require'.

Another way of inverting the factual enquiry model is to make extensive use of generalizations in nouns, adjectives and adverbs using, for example, nominalizations, comparatives and superlatives, and '-ly' type adverbs. Genie Laborde (1984), in her book *Influencing with Integrity*, calls these generalizations 'fat words' to distinguish them from 'lean' words, which are more specific. Nominalizations such as 'success', 'benefit', 'efficiency' and 'effectiveness' are fat words because they rely on listeners to develop their own deep structures, thereby giving individual meaning to the words. Words like 'computer', 'ledgers', and 'beer' are more specific and leave less to individual interpretation; they are therefore called lean words.

One of the techniques of 'persuading' is to use plenty of fat words and to say them in an enthusiastic manner. This is a technique well used by most politicians, who make speeches vague enough to be interpreted in a variety of different ways. Look carefully at this extract from a speech recently given by a politician –

> Clearly we shall have to work harder if we want to maintain the lifestyle we are all used to. We need to aim higher and be the best in everything we do. It is only by gaining commitment that we can ever hope to achieve the efficiency and effectiveness that will make us the best. Obviously I can't do it on my own; I need your help, your enthusiasm, your energy and, above all your willingness so that our productivity can be increased and our competitiveness improved.

This speech is full of nominalizations – 'lifestyle', 'commitment', 'efficiency', 'effectiveness', 'help', 'enthusiasm', 'energy', 'willingness', 'productivity' and 'competitiveness'. It also contains two '-ly' type adverbs, two comparatives and two superlatives. It is therefore very 'fat' – strong on rhetoric but weak on substance. Nonetheless, when delivered in a committed enthusiastic tone of voice, it was undoubtedly very effective in persuading and motivating a group of people.

Generalizations should not, however, be overdone, particularly in one-to-one interpersonal encounters. Where they are useful, though, is towards the end of the interaction, when a level of commitment is being sought and you want to persuade the other person that the agreed course of action is the best way to proceed. A short burst of fat words can then be very effective.

Repeated yes technique

Another technique that is often useful for generating persuasion patterns in the mind of the other person is the 'repeated yes' technique. This is frequently used by salespersons to assist them in making a 'close' but it can also be of value in one-to-one exchanges and general interactions. It comprises phrasing your words in such a way that the most likely response from the listener is 'yes'. By using a number of these responses in sequence, a 'yes set' is established in the other person and he is thereby put into a positive mind set.

Recently I was talking to a potential client. After discussing his problems for some time it was clear to me that an action-learning training programme might be just what he needed to meet many of his objectives. Towards the end of the discussions I proceeded as follows –

Me: It seems to me that your organization is disillusioned with conventional training programmes, right?

Client: Right.

Me: And do you find that your managers have difficulty in transferring what they have learned on the course to their actual jobs?

Client: We sure do.

Me: Is there too much academic input in your programmes and not enough emphasis on practical issues?

Client: Yes, that's one of the biggest complaints.

Me: Are you interested in hearing about a new training programme that is action-based, around real issues of concern to your organization?

Client: I'm all ears.

Me: One that is at the leading edge of training and development and is now being 'picked up' by most of the leading international companies.

Client: Come on, tell me about it.

By the end of this dialogue my client was almost sitting on the edge of his chair waiting for me to sell him an action-learning programme. It was then an easy matter to explain the product to him and a sale was made.

Looking at the above dialogue, you will see that all the responses made by me were couched in specific enquiry format so that the only possible answer that the client could make was 'yes'. Five times in a row I forced him to say 'yes' or its equivalent. The effect of this was to create a positive mind set in the client which encouraged him to look mainly at the positive side of what I was saying. In other words, he was conditioned by saying 'yes' to think favourably about the proposal.

There are two basic constructions to use when formulating 'yes' sets –

1 Formulate your response as a direct specific enquiry which will elicit a 'yes' from the other person. Do this by listening carefully to what has gone on earlier in the conversation and rephrasing it so that you know the answer will be 'yes'.
2 Make a statement that you know to be correct and turn it into a question by concluding it with phrases like –

   doesn't it?
   isn't it?
   OK?
   right?

9
How to give advice and handle criticism

As an example of psychoverbal communication in action, we shall examine here, in the final chapter, a problem which faces managers all over the world – how to give advice and handle criticism. Giving advice is one of the most difficult aspects of interpersonal communication, as the advice has to be given in a way that is accepted by the other person, otherwise barriers are created and the change process you require will never happen. Very often giving advice is interpreted as criticism, our defence barriers rise and the conversation degenerates into a non-productive, often vituperative dialogue. If either party views the conversation as giving or receiving 'criticism', then it is unlikely that anything positive will come from the discussion. Words must be phrased in such a way that both parties think of the exchange as 'giving advice' or 'receiving advice'.

How to give advice
The influencing skills model is an excellent framework to use for developing outstanding skills in giving advice. Basically there are four key points to remember and then it is a matter of practice.

Outcome matching
The only long-lasting change situations are those which can be defined as 'win–win'. This means that any advice-giving sessions should be structured in such a way that both parties gain a desired outcome. Too often as managers we set up win–lose situations where we 'win' (and are usually proud of it) and others 'lose'. Whilst in the short term we may get some benefit by having our immediate aims met, in the long term such a strategy will lead to lower morale and poorer performance. Therefore during an advice-giving session you need to spend time explaining to the

other person what benefits he will get out of the proposed change and also get his commitment to those benefits.

Pacing

Usually in a boss–subordinate appraisal or advice-giving situation the subordinate will be a little apprehensive or even 'on edge', and therefore it is most important that you spend time pacing the other person, particularly in the initial stages of the interaction. You will need to use sensory acuity here to look closely at how he is feeling, or perhaps you could just spend a minute imagining his situation and how you would be feeling if you were in his shoes. The pacing statements should then be loaded in favour of 'feelings' rather than 'facts'. Perhaps when learning the techniques you could concentrate on 1:2 or 1:3 fact/feeling loops which can be useful in these situations. For instance, a possible opening might be –

> Hi Jim, come in and sit down. Well it's time for the annual appraisal again – we've all been so busy it doesn't seem a year ago that we did the last one. Jim, I know you might feel a bit uneasy about what I might say. You've been disappointed during the year at the way some of the projects have turned out but I want to concentrate on the positive side of things and see how we can all make improvements for next year.

In another situation where you have called someone in to discuss an issue you might detect a hint of annoyance or aggressiveness which might prompt you to use 1:3 feeling/fact loops.

> Jim, I can see you're annoyed at my calling you in here. You're probably wondering what this is all about and think I'm taking up your valuable time. I know you've got deadlines to meet but in a few moments you'll see what I've got to say is important too.

This is primarily a pacing statement but you should also have recognized the leading phrase at the end which contains a presupposition and suggests that some important issues are about to be raised.

Focus on problem areas

When giving advice, there is a need to be problem-centred and to identify clearly and non-judgementally the areas where change is required. In order to do this well it is important to remember two things –

1 When describing areas where you consider improvements are required, never use general statements; always concentrate on 'the specific'. General statements will usually be viewed as direct criticism, for example –

You don't seem to pay enough attention to detail. Your performance is not up to our standards and you make frequent mistakes.

This response is full of generalizations and may well 'raise the hackles' on the other person, as people usually object to general critical comments. If your advice is to have a good chance of succeeding, it is important to use specific statements, giving specific facts of where you think things have gone wrong:

John, your last three reports have had significant errors on the output statistics. I would like to discuss these and find out why they are occurring.

If you present specific factual instances of problems that concern you and you have paced the other person well, you will find that the 'problem' has been separated from the 'people' and that through problem enquiry you will be able to extract important information in a non-threatening way.

2   Never be judgemental or evaluative when you are concentrating on the problem areas. It is so easy to impose our own values on the actions of others, particularly if they are subordinate to us. Examples of judgemental approaches would be –

You are too lazy . . .

You purposely undermined my authority on that occasion . . .

The words 'lazy' and 'purposely' are judgemental words in that they make a value judgement about particular behaviour. Perhaps poor performance has been interpreted as being lazy and the challenging of authority was evaluated as purposeful behaviour. Value judgements are dangerous because they involve a high degree of 'mind-reading'. If your mind-reading is inaccurate as it will invariably be in these cases then an immediate pacing interrupt will occur and the conversation is unlikely to proceed much further.

Leading

Once you have identified the problems surrounding the area you are concerned about and have obtained agreement from the other person that these are matters of importance, you can then lead him towards solutions by focusing on the positives. Rather than spend too much time talking about what not to do it is better to put your energies into positive, constructive feedback, concentrating on what might be done to improve performance. Rather than concentrate on the past it is better to focus on the future. People learn from their mistakes but only if you concentrate on how to prevent the mistakes from happening again rather than dissecting the negative aspects of how they happened and who was to blame.

Let's now see how some of these ideas might be put together. Consider part of an annual appraisal interview between Roger Smart and his boss Dick Holmes.

Holmes: Come in, Roger, and take a seat (pause). How do you feel things have gone in the last year? (Holmes and Smart sit next to each other around a low coffee table, not across the desk, which sometimes creates a formidable barrier. Holmes opens up with a general feeling enquiry which is often a good way to assess the situation so that you can decide on what pacing strategy to use.)

Smart: On the whole I think they have been fairly good, although, as you know, there have been one or two problems.

Holmes: Yes, Roger, I know you feel the Miles contract didn't go as well as it should have. Miles were a new account for us and it was important to do a good job because it could lead to work with their parent company. I can understand why you felt pressured and I hope you can understand why I 'flew off the handle' a few times. (Smart has used a generalization in the word 'problems' and, using problem enquiry, Holmes could have chosen to respond accordingly. However, he knows what Smart is referring to and decides to use a fact/feeling pacing loop.)

Smart: I know we've had our differences from time to time but I guess in the long run it's healthy for the business as it forces me to explore alternatives.

Holmes: In reviewing the last year perhaps it might be a good idea to start with the Miles contract and see how it could have been done better. (Holmes has jumped up into the leading sector to try and focus the discussion in on the Miles contract. Notice the presupposition in the last sentence.)

Smart: That's fine by me.

Holmes: What do you think were the main reasons we had difficulties?

Smart: Well, I'm not sure really.

Holmes: Do you think we allowed enough time for the job? (Holmes is still in the leading sector, trying to get Smart to focus in on the issues of priorities, time management and planning which he considers to be at the heart of the problem.)

Smart: Well in retrospect, no – I guess our planning phase was not all it might have been.

Holmes: What were the problems there? (Holmes drops down into problem enquiry, picking up on the generality 'not all it might have been'. Smart is now focused in on the issue of planning.)

Smart: Well, I guess the real problem is that I hate planning. I'm very much an action person – I do things first and worry about the consequences later.

Holmes: Yes, I've noticed too. Sometimes you remind me of a ball in a pinball machine 'rebounding' from one obstacle to another. (Holmes uses a leading diagnosis combined with a visual metaphor.)

Smart: (Laughing) Yes, I guess that's a pretty fair description.

Holmes: Have you ever thoght about taking steps to improve your management skills in this area? (Holmes uses simple leading.)

Smart: What can be done? I think I'm too old to change now.

Holmes: I was talking to our Training Manager last week and he says that there is a really good course on time management, priorities and planning at the Business School. Four of our people have been and the report-backs have been excellent. Each person has said they learned a lot which they could immediately apply. Would you like to attend?

Smart: Sure, if you think it will help me.

Holmes: Great, well I'll discuss it further with the Training Manager. Now let's look at one or two other issues . . .

How to handle criticism

Many managers are not skilled in giving advice and will only offer you criticism, sometimes in an aggressive manner. However, by using the principles of psychoverbal communication you can control their criticism and thereby control the situation. There are four basic aspects of psychoverbal communication that are important in this situation. Most of them have been discussed in previous chapters but it is useful to bring them here all together in one section. The four aspects are –

Pace the person criticizing.
Summarize regularly.
Specific enquiry.
Lead positively.

Pacing is always the fundamental technique to use in any interpersonal communication. If someone is starting to become aggressive with you, you should pace their tone and tempo and perhaps use some of the body-matching techniques mentioned in Chapter 4. However, you should not become aggressive yourself – remember you are pacing the process not the content. I have found the 101 per cent rule invaluable in these situations – find the 1 per cent of common ground (there is always something both parties agree on) and endorse it with 100 per cent of enthusiasm.

Summarizing regularly is especially useful if you are being criticized. It acts as a 'signpost' or collection point where you can clarify the areas being criticized so that both you and the other person have the same understanding of the situation. Under situations of stress, which always occur in encounters like this, people forget what has been said and do not always listen too closely. Summarizing regularly is a good way of keeping the discussion on track.

Specific enquiry is the way to deal with people who are making generalizations or being evaluative. You should ask them to give specific factual instances to back up their general comments. Follow the guide given in Chapter 5 on Enquiry, concentrating particularly on noun generalizations and incompletely specified verbs. It is important to gather the facts through problem enquiry before you give your opinion of the situation. Very often you will find that specific enquiry will defuse a situation, as the other person 'just can't think of an instance offhand'.

Positive leading is necessary when the other person is concentrating on the negatives, highlighting all the things you are doing wrong. In this situation it is a simple matter to turn the conversation around by using a simple leading phrase such as 'What do you suggest I do to improve things?' A question like this, if successful, will change the direction of the conversation and then you can concentrate on problem enquiry, insisting that the other person gives you specific advice on how your behaviour should be changed. If he is unable to do this, his criticism will usually dissipate and you will have the situation under control.

Let's look at some of these ideas in a dialogue between a Plant Engineer (Bob Neale) and the Works Engineer (Gary McLay). McLay has had a report that Neale held a meeting with the supervisors and plant operators and said they should refuse to work on the ammonia plant as it was unsafe. Apparently he also said that safety was a personal issue and management could not be held responsible for unsafe practices. McLay is furious about these contraventions of management practices and calls Neale in immediately to explain –

McLay: You bloody fool, who do you think you are – what right do you have to tell the operators that the ammonia plant is unsafe! It's caused all sorts of problems; we're behind schedule and need every bit of ammonia we can get and now the union has threatened a strike unless we take action. I've a good mind to sack you on the spot.

Neal (matching tone and tempo): Of course you're upset – we've got to meet the spring orders and we had that 'shut-down' only last month. I'd be upset too if what you said was correct but the fact is the ammonia plant is at this moment very unsafe. (Neale uses defusive pacing to 'lock into' McLay's state of mind.)

McLay: There is nothing wrong with the ammonia plant. It's all in perfect working order.

Neale: No it's not, the de-superheater line is clearly unsafe and could rupture any moment. (Neale focuses on specific facts.)

McLay: You told me about that last week – I said to build a protection box around that part which has got the pinhole leaks.

Neale: Look, the situation is as follows – I came to see you last week about the plant and told you that the superheater line had small leaks. You said that we couldn't shut down because we were behind schedule, right? Then you suggested a protection box as a possible temporary solution. On further inspection I decided that that solution was too dangerous for the fitters – in the process of installing it one of them could be hurt. I then asked you to come and inspect the line but you said you were too busy. (Neale summarizes the situation to date.)

McLay (slowing down now): That's correct.

Neale: How would you feel if there was a serious accident and someone was killed? (Neale now uses a combined leading/problem enquiry structure to paint a possible scenario if the plant continues to run.)

McLay: That won't happen.

Neale: How can you say that if you haven't come to see the extent of the problem? If you did, you would be able to examine the pipe and see the extent of the damage. You can hear the strange sound it is making and feel the weakness in the feeder flange. It's only logical that we should shut down and act immediately to avoid a catastrophe. (Neale uses a very effective combination of words designed to promote sensory saturation – 'see', 'hear', 'feel', 'logical', 'examine', 'act'.)

McLay: Hmmm! I didn't know it was that bad; perhaps we should go and look.

10

Developing your communication channels

The neurolinguistic model – the ‹V,A,K,O› model – defines a number of different communication channels. Excluding the olfactory channel there are eight important channels that are extremely useful in understanding how to influence others. These channels are summarized below:

Vi – internal visual channel

This channel describes the way people create images in their head. Some people think in pictures and find it quite easy to 'imaginate' and make connections through the generation of images. Communicating with these people in a way that stimulates their *internal visual channel* can be very effective.

Ve – external visual channel

This channel is associated with a focus on images that are generated from *external* sources. Some people have an ability to focus their visual awareness on images coming to them externally. These people are good observers and can take in quite detailed information. Communicating with these people in detailed diagrammatic form will help get your point of view across.

Ai – internal auditory channel

The auditory channel refers to sounds, tone and tempo. Those people who can readily focus on the *internal* channel will frequently recall situations by responding to the tone of discussions. Often they can detect subtle meanings through variation of tone.

Ae – external auditory channel

People who have this channel well developed respond well to sounds coming to them from *external* sources. They will respond to sounds with 'colour' and will be stimulated by well modulated enthusiastic tones. Likewise 'dull', slow sounds will cause their attention to wander.

Ki – the internal kinesthetic channel

The kinesthetic channel describes communication that is transmitted via the body. The *internal* channel refers to communications that are interpreted internally as 'feelings'. People who have this channel well developed often have a 'gut response' and are sometimes seen as 'intuitive'.

Ke – the external kinesthetic channel

This channel is preferred by people who like to communicate with their bodies. Such people are usually 'expressive' and can be quite active, often unable to sit still for long periods. Information can best be transmitted to them when they are using their bodies (walking, playing, eating, drinking, etc.).

Ad_i – the internal auditory digital channel

The auditory digital channel is the channel of people who like to process information in word form. The *internal* end of the channel is favoured by those people who have an *internal focus on words*. Such people will often run an *internal dialogue* where they constantly 'talk to themselves' as they receive, process and transmit information.

Ad_e – the external auditory digital channel

This channel describes people who find it easy to focus their awareness on words coming to them from external sources. Their attention span is usually quite long and in general they are excellent listeners.

It is less common for people to use all eight channels equally well. Most often people have three or four preferred ways of communicating and usually they favour one end of a channel continuum rather than the other. For example, people who find it easy to activate their *internal visual channel* often find it hard to focus on the *external visual channel*. Therefore they will be excellent at generating images but not so good at observing what is going on around them.

Likewise, some people are excellent at running an internal dialogue (*internal auditory digital channel*) but while they are doing this it is very difficult to focus on the *external auditory digital channel*, i.e., listening to the words that are being spoken to them.

Whatever channels you prefer to use in your communication, I have found that a marked increase in communication ability can occur when people try to develop those 'channels' which are less familiar to them. Concluder–producers who learn to develop their Vi channel often become far more creative and communicate more effectively with people from the 'exploring' part of the team management wheel. In return creator–innovators who learn to develop their Ve channel improve their data-gathering skills enormously and they communicate far more effectively with people from the 'controlling' part of the team management wheel.

Therefore, in this final chapter, we shall look at some of the exercises that you can do to sharpen up those channels which may be less familiar to you.

Learning how to 'imaginate'

For people in the 'organizer–controller' part of the team management wheel, activation of the Vi channel can be quite difficult. The best ways of learning how to do this are by the use of music and/or creative visualization.

Internal imaging is associated with a brainwave frequency in the range 8–12 cycles per second. This is commonly known as the *alpha* state. Certain types of music actually help the generation of alpha rhythms and a state of 'creative daydreaming' or internal visualization can be induced. The best 'class' of music to be used for this effect is known as 'sedative' music. Such music encourages a thoughtful or dreamlike mood because it lacks percussive rhythms and a strong underlying beat, and generally has legato melodic motives with repeticious, non-accentuated beats or unclear rhythmic pulses.

Sedative music is marketed by modern composers under the banner of *new age music*. One of the foremost pioneers of this type of music is Steve Halpern who believes that to generate a relaxed state, all semblance of a regular beat should be removed. This leaves spaces between the musical phrases and allows a meditative mood to develop, thereby increasing the alpha brainwave pattern in the consciousness of the listener. Much of this music uses repetitive superimposed arpeggios of major chords.

Music also seems to produce 'long range' memories and therefore the playing of sedative music as a background while gathering information or studying can aid in the storage of key data in the mind. This particular technique is used in *accelerated learning*.

If you are selecting music to stimulate alpha rhythms and thence help internal imaging the following guidelines will help you:

- The *rhythm* should be repetitious, lacking in pulse, unaccented and unpercussive in nature.
- The *pitch* should contain a characteristic drone quality over a medium range, together with a good proportion of high frequencies.
- The *melody* should have gaps between the phrases with legato motives and descending melodic contours.
- The *intervals* should be consonant, within the octave and using minor thirds and perfect fourths. Dissonance in general should be avoided.
- The *repetition* of melody or motives in a rhythmic and harmonic pattern is important.
- The *tempo* should be within 50–70 beats per minute.
- The *tone* should be rich in harmonics. String instruments, flutes and horns are particularly suitable.

There are many *new age* pieces which meet these requirements and one of my favourites is *Petals* played by Rising Sun (see References for further details)

Adagio and andante movements of the baroque era are also very effective. My favourite tape for generating internal images is a compilation of the following pieces played in this order:

Vivaldi	*Andante from Sinfonia in G, RV 149*
Mozart	*Andante from Piano Concerto No. 21, KV 467*
Albinoni	*Adagio for Strings in G Minor*
Telemann	*Andante from Flute Concerto in D*
Beethoven	*Piano Sonata in C# minor Opus 27 No. 2*
Gluck	*Allegro maestro from Don Juan*
Vivaldi	*Largo from Violin Concerto in D, Opus 11, No. 1*
Smetana	*Largo sostenuto from String Quartet No. 1*
Vivaldi	*The Four Seasons – Winter movement*

This sequence is very effective as it starts off at about 70 beats per minute and then slows down over the next few pieces to 50 beats per minute. Towards the end of the sequence the piece by Smetana introduces considerably more dissonance and, finally, *The Four Seasons* piece increases the rhythm and brings the listener back to a focused *beta* state where the brain rhythms speed up to the normal, alert, wakeful range of 18–40 cycles per second. Most people who have heard this sequence comment upon how restful it is and the increased ability they have to focus their attention on problems at hand after the sequence has finished.

To improve your internal imaging ability compile the indicated sequence leaving 5–10 seconds between each movement and play it once a day for a period of a week. The tape sequence will run for approximately 45 minutes. Remove all tight clothing and, if possible, relax in a hot bath before listening.

The music should be played loud so that you can feel the sound waves on your body and experience the external kinesthetic effect. Sit in a chair or lie on the floor and as the first piece plays breathe in to the beat of the music for four to six beats, hold your breath for four to six beats and then breathe out for four to six beats. Concentrate on your breathing for the first piece in the sequence, feeling the music flow over you and 'through' you.

Creative visualization

Creative visualization involves listening to someone else describe various scenes for you to visualize. It has to be carefully done using the right choice of words and also Ericksonian sequences which allow a light hypnotic effect to be induced. Ask someone to record the following word sequence (adapted from Charlesworth and Nathan, 1987) for you to listen to, or indeed use it with other people. It is best read with a background of new age music; my favourite piece for this reading is *Petals*. The words printed in bold should be analogue marked.

Sit comfortably in your chair and relax every muscle in your body. Slow your breathing down . . . breathing in for six counts . . . holding for six counts . . . and breathing out for six counts. . . .

As you listen to the sound of my voice I want you to picture yourself on a mountain top, high above a tropical rain forest on a small island. The morning rains have finished and the winds are carrying the clouds away. The sky is clear and blue and the warm tropical sun is shining. You can see below you the bright green trees in the rain forest. The raindrops on the leaves are reflecting the bright morning sun. You can see clearly the dense greenery interspersed with all those tropical flowers – look for them – the reds, the yellows, the pinks, the oranges. . . . In the far distance on the other side of the island you can see a line of coconut palms all along the sugar-white, sandy beach. Beyond that as far as the eye can see is crystal clear, brilliantly-blue water.

The sky is clear except for one small fluffy cloud that drifts alone in the gentle breeze until it is directly over you. Slowly this little cloud begins to sink down upon you. . . . It is a very pleasant feeling. . . . As the small fluffy cloud moves down across your face you feel the cool moist touch of it on your forehead and on your cheeks. As it moves down your body all tension slowly slips away and you find yourself letting go completely. The soft cloud moves across your shoulders, your chest and upper back and across your arms, as it brings with it a feeling of complete relaxation. It sinks down around your waist, your lower back, your hips and your legs. It moves down around you bringing with it a deep feeling of relaxation. Then the little cloud sinks underneath you and now you are floating on it. The cloud holds you perfectly and safely. It is a very pleasant feeling. . . . You are now lying back relaxed on this soft cloud. The warm tropical sun is shining. You can feel the warmth striking your body and still feel the soft moist touch of coolness on your face. You are feeling very very pleasant lying here supported by this soft white cloud. . . .

The little cloud now begins to drift downwind taking you on a journey. Here in your safe position on the cloud you can see the world going by below you. There is a gentle, pleasant, rocking motion as you drift along. All your cares and concerns are left behind you. The cloud is magic and can take you any place you want to go. . . .

In the far distance you can see a delightful green valley. The valley is between some gentle sloping mountains. This is a place where you can be completely at peace and totally happy. Gradually the fluffy cloud takes you drifting **down** and **down** through the sky to this beautiful place. You move **down** . . . **down** . . . into the valley, and the cloud gently comes to the ground and stops. You get off the cloud in this beautiful place, completely at peace. . . . Take some time to look around this fresh green valley. . . . Now you can see a lake. . . . Listen to the birds. . . . Feel the sun shining on you. . . . It is springtime. . . . Smell the scent in the air.

The water is just barely lapping along the shore of the lake. You see a small boat tied there. Now you enter the boat, untie it and drift out into the lake. In the bottom of the boat are some soft blankets for you to lie down on. Now you are floating in the quiet shallow lake. The boat is rocking gently from the motion of the water as it drifts on . . . and on. . . . How relaxing the rocking and massaging is. The boat carries you along out into the open. Feel again the warm sunlight and the soft breeze as you drift along. You feel relaxed and calm and peaceful. The gentle rocking motion of the boat as you lie there massages you with feelings of peace. Your state of relaxation becomes **deeper** as the boat gently moves too and fro. . . . Now you drift **deeper** and **deeper** into your relaxed state.

As you continue to drift you become aware of the sounds of nature – the soft breeze, the lapping water, and the birds and the animals along the shore. . . . Smell the grass and flowers as the breeze brings you their pleasant scents. You are lazily drifting **deeper** and **deeper** into a profound feeling of peace and pleasantness until very slowly and gently the boat washes up against the shore. You remain in a very complete state of total relaxation. . . .

Now you get out of the boat and take the soft blanket with you and lie down beneath a large willow tree growing on the green bank beside the lake. You notice a small silver box under the willow tree. Inside it is a piece of paper folded in half. On it is written an important message for you – one that is very important to your future. I wonder what it says. . . .

As you lie on your blanket on the thick green grass you see your soft white fluffy cloud in the distance coming towards you. It hovers over you and gently begins to sink down. . . . Again feel that pleasant delightful feeling as the small cloud moves down across your face. You can feel the cool, moist touch of it on your forehead and on your cheeks. As it again descends all tensions dissolve away . . . away from your shoulders and neck, your chest, your arms . . . feel the wave of relaxation as the cloud descends down past your waist, your lower back, your hips and your legs. The little cloud sinks underneath you and soon you are floating on it, once again feeling safe, relaxed and pleasant.

The cloud now begins to rise, taking you with it, drifting with the wind. . . . This time you are going on a journey of great importance . . . **back down** through the years of your life . . . as far as you can go. . . . Here from the safety and comfort of your soft fluffy cloud you can review and relive those past times of your life when you felt particularly **strong** and **powerful** . . . times when you were **confident** in everything you did. Review now each and every special moment . . . moments when you felt particularly **proud** of what you have achieved and accomplished. Enjoy these moments which can energize and refresh you. Pause at those times which are particularly pleasurable to you . . . times you can recall with fond memories . . . some of which you may have forgotten but which now come back to you as you relive for as long as you want those past experiences when you felt strong, **happy, powerful, confident** and **effective**. Draw energy from each and every experience. Let your soft, safe cloud take you **back** . . . **back** . . . down the years wherever it wants to go. **Down, down** as far as it can. Savour all these moments and learn from them. . . .

Now it is time for your cloud to make its return journey up through the years, getting older and older, growing back to the age you are now but bringing with you those feelings of power and confidence and strength.

Your little fluffy cloud can always be a source of relaxation and pleasure and strength and comfort to you. Now that you have experienced the deep relaxation this cloud can bring to you it will become your ally, always available to help you when you need to relax. To remove stress just take a deep breath and as you breathe out, see your fluffy white cloud overhead. Slowly this little cloud will then begin to sink down around you and you will feel the wave of relaxation pass over you . . . pass down your forehead, your neck, across your shoulders, your chest, your upper back and across your arms, as it brings with it a feeling of relaxation and power. It will sink down across your waist, your lower back, your hips, and your legs causing a total release of all tension held within you. Your cloud is your companion, your friend, your ally – it can always take you wherever you want.

Now we are nearly at the end of our journey. Soon I will count to three. As you take a deep breath silently say each number to yourself. When you reach three you can open your eyes and you will be refreshed, relaxed and alert. When you open your eyes you will find yourself back in the real world but now the world will seem slower and more calm and you will be relaxed and peaceful. . . . **One** –relaxed but more alert, **two** – mentally wide awake, **three** – eyes open, alert and refreshed.

Sharpening-up your Ve (external visual) channel

Typically people from the creator–innovator/explorer–promoter part of the team management wheel have difficulty in activating their external visual channel for long periods. They may try to concentrate on 'observing' but often their mind 'wanders' as they generate internal pictures. These internal images cause the Ve channel to be attenuated and external visual data is lost.

I have carried out experiments in observation skills with various groups of people on management development workshops for a number of years now. There is no doubt in my mind that in general, concluder–producers and controller–inspectors make the best observers. I first noticed this some years ago when running a safety management programme for a large chemical company. The emphasis in this programme was on introducing 'team safety auditing' where process workers would regularly audit 'unsafe practices' in the plant by conducting a regular safety review. The theory was that there is a relationship between unsafe practices and 'loss time injuries' and 'medical treatment injuries'. By reducing the unsafe practices then control over the injuries is possible. In this programme I noticed that when operating in a group, the creator–innovator/explorer–promoters always observed significantly fewer 'unsafe practices' compared with people from the other side of the team management wheel.

Many human resource professionals involved in training and development map into the creator–innovator/explorer–promoter sectors of the wheel and therefore they sometimes have difficulty with their observation skills. You will recall earlier in the book I mentioned that 'sensory acuity', particularly visual acuity, is very important in gathering 'nonverbal' information about the other person. Good sensory acuity enables you to immediately detect when other people are not listening to you and also to get feedback on the effect that your message is having. These skills are obviously of paramount importance when teaching or facilitating workshops. Sometimes the creator–innovator/explorer–promoter facilitator gets 'carried away' with an idea and is unaware that he has 'lost' the audience. This is usually because the Vi channel has been activated and therefore the Ve channel is attenuated.

In order to develop the external visual channel it is necessary to learn to control the generation of internal images. This means focusing all your visual awareness externally and concentrating on looking at fine details. To prevent the Vi channel from 'switching on', try activating your internal auditory digital channel (Ad_i). Select an object to look at – a scene, people, shops, etc. and then run an internal dialogue as you talk to yourself about what you are seeing. This procedure should be done for 5 or 10 minutes each day, whenever you have time. Try doing it whenever you go walking. It will open up a new dimension for you in the world of nature.

For those of you who are teachers or 'trainers' try doing this with the people on your workshop. Look closely at each person, noting any unusual feature about them, whenever you get an opportunity in the workshop. Try regularly scanning the group for a few seconds every few minutes to make sure they are still attentive. If they are not, then engage in some form of pattern interruption. In this way your Vi channel can have precedence, but there is almost an 'inbuilt' programme for the Vi channel to be temporarily interrupted by the Ve channel. This 'cycling' feature between the two ends of the visual channel can be very effective in developing all-round good visual skills.

Controlling the auditory digital channel

People who map into the assessor–developer/thruster–organizer part of the team management wheel often find it easy to activate their internal auditory digital channel (Ad_i). It is very easy for them to switch on their internal dialogue and run a commentary on what others are saying. They will analyse the information, develop solutions and prepare their reply, all while the other person is talking. Unfortunately while the Ad_i channel is activated, the Ad_e (external auditory digital) channel is attenuated and therefore they are not always the best listeners. People with a strong Ad_i channel often have difficulty 'switching off'. They sometimes suffer from insomnia because a whole 'inner world' of activity prevents them from sleeping.

Now the Adi channel is very important for analytical decision-making but in order to be a good communicator you must know when to switch it on and off. People with a strong propensity for internal dialogue need to work hard at controlling this channel and can benefit from learning the technique of *stopping the world*.

Stopping the world is a term coined by Carlos Castaneda in his books about Don Juan (see Journey to Ixtlan, Chapter 13) and refers to the ability to shut down all internal processing and focus awareness entirely on external data. It takes a little while to learn how to do it but once mastered it is therapeutic and 're-energizes' your total awareness.

Tai Chi or other similar disciplines can also assist in 'stopping the world' The 'sets' of Tai Chi require such concentration, such focusing on the external kinesthetic channel that the internal auditory digital channel shuts down. This why people find such techniques so relaxing.

Simple meditation can also achieve the same effect. Sit in a position where you are comfortable, and focus your vision on a blank spot in front of you. Concentrate on observing through your *peripheral vision.* Notice any movement that might be occurring at the periphery. You will find after a while that your *foveal* (central) vision becomes fatigued and you will enter a state of inner silence. It sometimes helps if you initially listen to all the sounds around you, trying to identify each and every one, no matter how far away. Also scan your body, checking each muscle group to 'feel' its state. In this way your awareness is totally preoccupied on external events and there is no opportunity for an internal dialogue to commence. This technique employed once a day for 10–20 minutes can be extremely beneficial in giving you control over the valuable, but sometimes interfering internal auditory digital channel.

Once you have learned how to switch off your internal dialogue you will find that your ability to listen is enhanced. If your mind starts to wander when someone is talking to you then mentally 'flick a switch' in your head turning off your internal auditory digital channel. Focus your vision on their eyes and take in every word, repeating it internally if necessary, to make sure that you have exacted the correct meaning. With practice you can flick your auditory digital switch from internal to external at a moment's notice – listening and processing, listening and processing but never both at the same time.

People from the reporter–adviser/upholder–maintainer part of the wheel tend to be naturally gifted at listening because of a preference to activate their external auditory digital channel. Because they are also internal kinesthetic people they will often interpret information through their belief frameworks and 'intuitively' react to situations. If you are like this then it might be of benefit for you to practice activating your internal auditory digital channel. When people say things to you that generate strong feelings from within, then switch on your internal dialogue and try to analyse why you have these feelings. Are they justified? What has caused you to react in the way you have?

Kinesthetic channels

People from the assessor–developer and thruster–organizer sectors of the team management wheel often have a strong external kinesthetic channel and therefore they like experiencing situations through their body. Often they are very active people who sometimes find it difficult to sit still. Because they tend to also use the internal auditory digital channel quite a lot they sometimes may 'over-analyse' situations. If this is the case for you then it may help if you try to get in touch with your inner feelings about various situations. Sometimes people ignore or devalue this important way or transmitting and receiving information. Frequently ask yourself, 'How am I feeling? Am I happy, sad, annoyed, frustrated etc.?'. In this way you can develop an awareness and sensitivity for the internal kinesthetic channel.

Auditory channels

People with an orientation towards the external auditory channel are sensitive to sounds coming to them from external sources. If enthusiastic tones are used, they often become enthusiastic. If melancholy tones are used then they sometimes become melancholy. Therefore you can often have an influence upon their mood just by the tone and tempo of your delivery. However they do not 'analyse' these sounds but simply respond to them unconsciously.

If you are from the controller–inspector/concluder–producer part of the team management wheel you may not respond as dynamically to the external auditory digital channel as people from the other side of the Wheel. If this is the case then it may be worth developing this channel. Experiment with varying the speed at which you talk, speeding up or slowing down to 'mark' appropriate moods. Try different modulations and note their effect.

Likewise allow yourself to respond to the moods generated by other people's use of the Ae channel. As people talk to you quickly analyse the effect their sounds are having on you. If they sound enthusiastic then think about becoming enthusiastic too. If they are 'sad' then generate these feelings in yourself. In this way you will be improving your 'pacing' skills.

In conclusion

In this book I have presented the techniques of psychoverbal communication in a somewhat 'clinical' form as I believe this treatment is necessary so that the complex processes of communication can be structured into an easily learnable format. Many current texts on communication are full of hints and anecdotes, and, while interesting and entertaining to read, do little in the way of instructing people in how to be really influential with their colleagues at work.

Therefore, I have developed the seven-stage influencing skills model as a cognitive aid to 'chunk down' complex communication patterns into 'bite-sized' pieces so as to help you become a really proficient communicator. In fact I recommend that you concentrate on each sector of the model for days at a time, weaving the various techniques presented here into your normal daily conversations until you become comfortable with their use. Start with the 'pacing' ideas and slowly work your way through the problem-centred techniques, around to the techniques of 'leading', 'proposing' and 'persuading'.

However, in using the techniques it is not my intention that you should act like a 'scientist', experimenting with people in a clinical way so as to influence them against their will. These techniques are undoubtedly very powerful and in using them you have a responsibility to act ethically and with integrity. In all communication interactions on major issues try to set up 'win–win' situations, whereby the other person gains from the interaction, in addition to achieving your goals. 'Win–lose' situations may seem justified in the short term but you could be in danger of 'winning the battle but losing the war'. If you act to manipulate people, you will soon get a reputation as a person 'out for his own ends', and then no amount of skills in communication can 'win back the lost ground'.

To put some of the skills discussed here into practice it may be worth attending the various three-day influencing skills workshops that are run by various TMS distributors. Please contact the organizations listed at the end of this book if you would like more information about TMS in your country.

References

Bandler, Richard and Grinder, John, *Patterns of the Hypnotic Techniques of Milton H. Erickson, M.D.*, Volume 1, MetaPublications, Cupertino, California 95014, 1975.

Bandler, Richard and Grinder, John, *The Structure of Magic*, Vol. 1, Science and Behaviour Books, Palo Alto, California 94306, 1975.

Castaneda, C., *Journey to Ixtlan*, Penguin Books, London, 1972.

Charlesworth, E. A. and Nathan, R. G., *Stress Management – A Comprehensive Guide to Wellness*, Corgi Books, London, 1987.

Chomsky, N., *Syntactic Structures*, Mouton, The Hague, 1957.

Chomsky, N., *Aspects of the Theory of Syntax*, MIT Press, Cambridge, Mass., 1965.

Davies, R. V., *The Team Management Index Manual for Licensed Users*, MCB University Press, Bradford, 1988.

Fast, J., *Body Language*, Pan Books, London and Sydney, 1972.

Grinder, John and Bandler, Richard, *The Structure of Magic*, Vol. 2, Science and Behaviour Books, Palo Alto, California 94306, 1976.

Grinder, John, DeLozier, Judith and Bandler, Richard, *Patterns of the Hypnotic Techniques of Milton H. Erickson, M.D.*, Volume 2, Meta Publications, Cupertino, California 95014, 1977.

Haley, J. *Uncommon Therapy*, W. W. Norton, New York, 1973.

Jung, C. J., *Psychological Types*, Volume 6, *The Collected Works of C. J. Jung*, Routledge and Kegan Paul, London, 1971. First published in 1923.

King, M., Novik, L. and Citrenbaum, C., *Irresistible Communication*, W. B. Saunders, Philadelphia, PA 19105, 1983.

Laborde, Genie, *Influencing with Integrity*, Syntony Publishing, 1450 Byron St., Palo Alto, California 94301, 1984.

Maier, N. R. F., *Problem-solving Discussions and Conferences*, McGraw-Hill Management Series, 1963.

Margerison, C. J., *Managerial Problem-solving*, McGraw-Hill, 1974.

Margerison, C. J., *Conversational Control Skills for Managers*, W. H. Allen Mercury Books, 1987.

Margerison C. J. and McCann, D. J., *The Team Management Index*, MCB University Press, 1984.

Margerison, C. J. and McCann, D. J., "Team Mapping – A New Approach to Managerial Leadership', *Journal of European Industrial Training*, Vol. 8, No. 1, 1984.

Margerison, C. J., McCann, D. J. and Davies, R. V., 'The Margerison–McCann Team Management Resource – Theory and Applications', *International Journal of Manpower*, Vol. 7, No. 2, 1986.

Margerison, C. J. and McCann, D. J., *Team Management – Practical New Approaches*, Mercury Books, 1990.

Pease, Allan, *Body Language*, Sheldon Press, London, 1984.

Rising Sun (Marcus Allen, Jon Bernoff, Dallas Smith, Teja Bell), *Petals*, Narada Publishing, PB6037, 2001 Ha Haarlem, Holland.

Sculley John, with Byrne John, *Odyssey – Pepsi to Apple . . . A Journey of Adventure, Ideas and the Future*, Harper and Row, New York, 1987.

Team Management Systems

Team Management Systems is a suite of products developed by Dick McCann and Charles Margerison, to improve individual and team performance at work. It comprises the *team management index*, the *types of work index*, the *linking skills index* and the *influencing skills index*.

Of relevance to this book are the team management index and the influencing skills index. The team management index is a sixty-item questionnaire that measures your work preferences. It maps you on to the team management wheel and produces a 4000-word report on work preferences, leadership skills, decision-making, and teamwork.

The influencing skills index is a forty-item questionnaire that measures behavioural characteristics about another person. The index is processed and a 3000 word report generated giving you advice on how to influence this person. The report focuses on the seven influencing skills of *pacing*, *enquiry*, *diagnosing*, *summarizing*, *leading*, *proposing* and *persuading*.

If you would like to complete either of these indexes or find out more about Team Management Systems then please contact one of the following organizations:

United Kingdom, Europe and general enquiries
Ms Cathy Hick
TMS(UK) Ltd
Water Meadows
367 Huntington Road
York YO3 9HR
ENGLAND
Telephone: (0904) 641640
Fax: (0904) 640076

Australia, South East Asia, South Pacific
Ms Heather Burnett
Team Management Resources
PO Box 709
Toowong
Brisbane
Australia 4069
Telephone: (07) 870 2580
Fax: (07) 870 4013

New Zealand
Dr Paul Robinson
Team Management Services
PO Box 21–194
Henderson
Auckland
New Zealand
Telephone: (09) 832 3256

Index